The *New* Daily Study Bible

The Letter to the
Hebrews

The *New* Daily Study Bible

The Letter to the
Hebrews

William Barclay

Westminster John Knox Press
LOUISVILLE • LONDON

First edition published in 1955 as *The Daily Study Bible: The Letter to the Hebrews*
Revised edition published in 1976
This third edition fully revised and updated by Saint Andrew Press and published
as *The New Daily Study Bible: The Letter to the Hebrews* in 2002

Published in the United States by
Westminster John Knox Press
Louisville, Kentucky

Cover design by McColl Productions Ltd, by courtesy of Saint Andrew Press

Typeset by Waverley Typesetters, Galashiels

PRINTED IN THE UNITED STATES OF AMERICA

06 07 08 09 10 11 12 — 10 9 8 7 6 5 4 3

Library of Congress Cataloging-in-Publication Data is on file at the Library of
Congress, Washington, D.C.

ISBN-13: 978-0-664-22558-2
ISBN-10: 0-664-22558-6

To D.A.

FOR ALL HIS MANY KINDNESSES TO ME

AND ESPECIALLY

BECAUSE IT WAS AT HIS REQUEST

THAT I WROTE THIS BOOK

CONTENTS

HEBREWS

SERIES FOREWORD
(by Ronnie Barclay)

My father always had a great love for the English language
and its literature. As a student at the University of Glasgow,
he won a prize in the English class – and I have no doubt
that he could have become a Professor of English instead
of Divinity and Biblical Criticism. In a pre-computer age, he
had a mind like a computer that could store vast numbers of
quotations, illustrations, anecdotes and allusions; and, more
remarkably still, he could retrieve them at will. The editor of
this revision has, where necessary, corrected and attributed
the vast majority of these quotations with considerable skill
and has enhanced our pleasure as we read quotations from
Plato to T. S. Eliot.

There is another very welcome improvement in the new
text. My mother was one of five sisters, and my grandmother
was a commanding figure as the Presbyterian minister's
wife in a small village in Ayrshire in Scotland. She ran that
small community very efficiently, and I always felt that my
father, surrounded by so many women, was more than some-
what overawed by it all! I am sure that this is the reason why
his use of English tended to be dominated by the words 'man',
'men' and so on, with the result that it sounded very male-
orientated. Once again, the editor has very skilfully improved
my father's English and made the text much more readable
for all of us by amending the often one-sided language.

It is a well-known fact that William Barclay wrote at break-
neck speed and never corrected anything once it was on

paper – he took great pride in mentioning this at every possible opportunity! This revision, in removing repetition and correcting the inevitable errors that had slipped through, has produced a text free from all the tell-tale signs of very rapid writing. It is with great pleasure that I commend this revision to readers old and new in the certainty that William Barclay speaks even more clearly to us all with his wonderful appeal in this new version of his much-loved *Daily Study Bible*.

Ronnie Barclay
Bedfordshire
2001

GENERAL INTRODUCTION

(by William Barclay, from the 1975 edition)

The Daily Study Bible series has always had one aim – to convey the results of scholarship to the ordinary reader. A. S. Peake delighted in the saying that he was a 'theological middle-man', and I would be happy if the same could be said of me in regard to these volumes. And yet the primary aim of the series has never been academic. It could be summed up in the famous words of Richard of Chichester's prayer – to enable men and women 'to know Jesus Christ more clearly, to love him more dearly, and to follow him more nearly'.

It is all of twenty years since the first volume of *The Daily Study Bible* was published. The series was the brain-child of the late Rev. Andrew McCosh, MA, STM, the then Secretary and Manager of the Committee on Publications of the Church of Scotland, and of the late Rev. R. G. Macdonald, OBE, MA, DD, its Convener.

It is a great joy to me to know that all through the years *The Daily Study Bible* has been used at home and abroad, by minister, by missionary, by student and by layman, and that it has been translated into many different languages. Now, after so many printings, it has become necessary to renew the printer's type and the opportunity has been taken to restyle the books, to correct some errors in the text and to remove some references which have become outdated. At the same time, the Biblical quotations within the text have been changed to use the Revised Standard Version, but my own original translation of the New Testament passages has been retained at the beginning of each daily section.

There is one debt which I would be sadly lacking in courtesy if I did not acknowledge. The work of revision and correction has been done entirely by the Rev. James Martin, MA, BD, Minister of High Carntyne Church, Glasgow. Had it not been for him this task would never have been undertaken, and it is impossible for me to thank him enough for the selfless toil he has put into the revision of these books.

It is my prayer that God may continue to use *The Daily Study Bible* to enable men better to understand His word.

William Barclay
Glasgow
1975
(Published in the 1975 edition)

GENERAL FOREWORD

(by John Drane)

I only met William Barclay once, not long after his retirement from the chair of Biblical Criticism at the University
of Glasgow. Of course I had known about him long before
that, not least because his theological passion – the Bible –
was also a significant formative influence in my own life
and ministry. One of my most vivid memories of his influence goes back to when I was working on my own doctoral
research in the New Testament. It was summer 1971, and I
was a leader on a mission team working in the north-east of
Scotland at the same time as Barclay's Baird Lectures were
being broadcast on national television. One night, a young
Ph.D. scientist who was interested in Christianity, but still
unsure about some things, came to me and announced: 'I've
just been watching William Barclay on TV. He's convinced
me that I need to be a Christian; when can I be baptized?'
That kind of thing did not happen every day. So how could it
be that Barclay's message was so accessible to people with
no previous knowledge or experience of the Christian faith?

I soon realised that there was no magic ingredient that
enabled this apparently ordinary professor to be a brilliant
communicator. His secret lay in who he was, his own sense
of identity and purpose, and above all his integrity in being
true to himself and his faith. Born in the far north of Scotland,
he was brought up in Motherwell, a steel-producing town
south of Glasgow where his family settled when he was only
five, and this was the kind of place where he felt most at

home. Though his association with the University of Glasgow provided a focus for his life over almost fifty years, from his first day as a student in 1925 to his retirement from the faculty in 1974, he never became an ivory-tower academic, divorced from the realities of life in the real world. On the contrary, it was his commitment to the working-class culture of industrial Clydeside that enabled him to make such a lasting contribution not only to the world of the university but also to the life of the Church.

He was ordained to the ministry of the Church of Scotland at the age of twenty-six, but was often misunderstood even by other Christians. I doubt that William Barclay would ever have chosen words such as 'missionary' or 'evangelist' to describe his own ministry, but he accomplished what few others have done, as he took the traditional Presbyterian emphasis on spirituality-through-learning and transformed it into a most effective vehicle for evangelism. His own primary interest was in the history and language of the New Testament, but William Barclay was never only a historian or literary critic. His constant concern was to explore how these ancient books, and the faith of which they spoke, could continue to be relevant to people of his own time. If the Scottish churches had known how to capitalize on his enormous popularity in the media during the 1960s and 1970s, they might easily have avoided much of the decline of subsequent years.

Connecting the Bible to life has never been the way to win friends in the world of academic theology, and Barclay could undoubtedly have made things easier for himself had he been prepared to be a more conventional academic. But he was too deeply rooted in his own culture – and too seriously committed to the gospel – for that. He could see little purpose in a belief system that was so wrapped up in arcane and complicated terminology that it was accessible only to experts. Not only did he demystify Christian theology, but he also did it for working people, addressing the kind of things that mattered to ordinary folks in their everyday lives. In doing so, he also challenged the elitism that has often been deeply ingrained in the twin worlds of academic theology and the Church, with their shared assumption that popular culture is an inappropriate vehicle for serious thinking. Professor Barclay can hardly have been surprised when his predilection for writing books for the masses – not to mention talking to them on television – was questioned by his peers and even occasionally dismissed as being 'unscholarly' or insufficiently 'academic'. That was all untrue, of course, for his work was soundly based in reliable scholarship and his own extensive knowledge of the original languages of the Bible. But like One many centuries before him (and unlike most of his peers, in both Church and academy), 'the common people heard him gladly' (Mark 12:37), which no doubt explains why his writings are still inspirational – and why it is a particular pleasure for me personally to commend them to a new readership in a new century.

John Drane
University of Aberdeen
2001

EDITOR'S PREFACE

(by Linda Foster)

When the first volume of the original *Daily Bible Readings*, which later became *The Daily Study Bible* (the commentary on Acts), was published in 1953, no one could have anticipated or envisaged the revolution in the use of language which was to take place in the last quarter of the twentieth century. Indeed, when the first revised edition, to which William Barclay refers in his General Introduction, was completed in 1975, such a revolution was still waiting in the wings. But at the beginning of the twenty-first century, inclusive language and the concept of political correctness are well-established facts of life. It has therefore been with some trepidation that the editing of this unique and much-loved text has been undertaken in producing *The New Daily Study Bible*. Inevitably, the demands of the new language have resulted in the loss of some of Barclay's most sonorous phrases, perhaps best remembered in the often-repeated words 'many a man'. Nonetheless, this revision is made in the conviction that William Barclay, the great communicator, would have welcomed it. In the discussion of Matthew 9:16–17 ('The Problem of the New Idea'), he affirmed the value of language that has stood the test of time and in which people have 'found comfort and put their trust', but he also spoke of 'living in a changing and expanding world' and questioned the wisdom of reading God's word to twentieth-century men and women in Elizabethan English. It is the intention of this new edition to heed that warning and to bring

William Barclay's message of God's word to readers of the twenty-first century in the language of their own time.

In the editorial process, certain decisions have been made in order to keep a balance between that new language and the familiar Barclay style. Quotations from the Bible are now taken from the New Revised Standard Version, but William Barclay's own translation of individual passages has been retained throughout. Where the new version differs from the text on which Barclay originally commented, because of the existence of an alternative reading, the variant text is indicated by square brackets. I have made no attempt to guess what Barclay would have said about the NRSV text; his commentary still refers to the Authorized (King James) and Revised Standard Versions of the Bible, but I believe that the inclusive language of the NRSV considerably assists the flow of the discussion.

For similar reasons, the dating conventions of BC and AD – rather than the more recent and increasingly used BCE (before the common era) and CE (common era) – have been retained. William Barclay took great care to explain the meanings of words and phrases and scholarly points, but it has not seemed appropriate to select new terms and make such explanations on his behalf.

One of the most difficult problems to solve has concerned monetary values. Barclay had his own system for translating the coinage of New Testament times into British currency. Over the years, these equivalent values have become increasingly out of date, and often the force of the point being made has been lost or diminished. There is no easy way to bring these equivalents up to date in a way that will continue to make sense, particularly when readers come from both sides of the Atlantic. I have therefore followed the only known yardstick that gives any feel for the values concerned, namely that a *denarius* was a day's wage for a working man, and I have made alterations to the text accordingly.

One of the striking features of *The Daily Study Bible* is the range of quotations from literature and hymnody that are used by way of illustration. Many of these passages appeared without identification or attribution, and for the new edition I have attempted wherever possible to provide sources and authors. In the same way, details have been included about scholars and other individuals cited, by way of context and explanation, and I am most grateful to Professor John Drane for his assistance in discovering information about some of the more obscure or unfamiliar characters. It is clear that readers use *The Daily Study Bible* in different ways. Some look up particular passages while others work through the daily readings in a more systematic way. The descriptions and explanations are therefore not offered every time an individual is mentioned (in order to avoid repetition that some may find tedious), but I trust that the information can be discovered without too much difficulty.

Finally, the 'Further Reading' lists at the end of each volume have been removed. Many new commentaries and individual studies have been added to those that were the basis of William Barclay's work, and making a selection from that ever-increasing catalogue is an impossible task. It is nonetheless my hope that the exploration that begins with these volumes of *The New Daily Study Bible* will go on in the discovery of new writers and new books.

Throughout the editorial process, many conversations have taken place – conversations with the British and American publishers, and with those who love the books and find in them both information and inspiration. Ronnie Barclay's contribution to this revision of his father's work has been invaluable. But one conversation has dominated the work, and that has been a conversation with William Barclay himself through the text. There has been a real sense of listening to his voice in all the questioning and in the searching for new words to convey the meaning of that text. The aim of *The New Daily Study Bible* is to make clear his message, so that the distinctive voice, which has spoken to so many in past years, may continue to be heard for generations to come.

Linda Foster
London
2001

INTRODUCTION TO
THE LETTER TO THE HEBREWS

God Fulfils Himself in Many Ways

Religion has never been the same thing to everyone. 'God', as Tennyson said in *Mort d'Arthur*, 'fulfils himself in many ways.' The Irish writer George Russell said: 'There are as many ways of climbing to the stars as there are people to climb.' There is a saying which tells us very truly and very beautifully that 'God has his own secret stairway into every heart.' Broadly speaking, there have been four great conceptions of religion.

(1) To some, it is *inward fellowship with God.* It is a union with Christ so close and so intimate that Christians can be said to live in Christ and Christ to live in them. That was Paul's conception of religion. To him, it was something which mystically united him with God.

(2) To some, religion is what gives us *a standard for life and a power to reach that standard.* On the whole, that is what religion was to James and to Peter. It was something which showed them what life ought to be and which enabled them to attain it.

(3) To some, religion is *the highest satisfaction of their minds.* Their minds seek and seek until they find that they can rest in God. It was Plato who said that 'the unexamined life is the life not worth living'. There are some people who have to understand things in order to make sense of life. On

the whole, that is what religion was to John. The first chapter of his gospel is one of the greatest attempts in the world to state religion in a way that really satisfies the mind.

(4) To some, religion is *access to God.* It is that which removes the barriers and opens the door to his living presence. That is what religion was to the writer of the Letter to the Hebrews. His mind was dominated with that idea. He found in Christ the one person who could take him into the very presence of God. His whole idea of religion is summed up in the great passage in Hebrews 10:19–22:

> Therefore, my friends, since we have confidence to enter the sanctuary by the blood of Jesus, by the new and living way that he opened for us through the curtain (that is, through his flesh) . . . let us approach with a true heart in full assurance of faith.

If the writer to the Hebrews had one text, it was: '*Let us draw near.*'

The Double Background

The writer to the Hebrews had a double background, and this idea fitted into both sides. He had a *Greek background.* Ever since the time of Plato, 500 years before, the Greeks had been occupied in their thinking by the contrast between the real and the unreal, the seen and the unseen, things that exist in time and things that are eternal. It was the Greek idea that somewhere there was a real world of which this was only a shadowy and imperfect copy. Plato had the idea that somewhere there was a world of perfect *forms* or *ideas* or *patterns*, of which everything in this world was an imperfect copy. To take a simple instance, somewhere there was laid up the pattern of a perfect chair of which all the chairs in this world were inadequate copies. Plato said: 'The Creator of the world had designed and carried out his work according to an unchangeable and eternal pattern of which the world is only a copy.' The Jewish thinker Philo, who took his ideas from Plato, said: 'God knew from the beginning that a fair copy could never come into being apart from a fair pattern; and that none of the objects perceivable by sense could be flawless which was not modelled after an archetype and spiritual idea, and thus, when he prepared to create this visible world, he shaped beforehand the ideal world in order to constitute the corporeal after the incorporeal and godlike pattern.' When the Roman statesman Cicero was talking of the laws that people know and use on earth, he said: 'We have no real and life-like likeness of real law and genuine justice; all we enjoy is a shadow and a sketch.'

The thinkers of the ancient world all had this idea that somewhere there is a real world of which this one is only a kind of imperfect copy. Here, we can only guess and feel our way; here, we can work only with copies and imperfect things. But, in the unseen world, there are the real and perfect things. When the great churchman John Henry Newman died, they erected a statue to him, and on the pedestal of it are the Latin words: *Ab umbris et imaginibus ad veritatem*, 'Away from the shadows and the semblances to the truth.' If that is so, clearly the great task of this life is to get away from the shadows and the imperfections and to reach *reality*. This is exactly what the writer to the Hebrews claims that Jesus Christ can enable us to do. To the Greeks, the writer to the Hebrews said: 'All your lives, you have been trying to get from the shadows to the truth. That is just what Jesus Christ can enable you to do.'

The Jewish Background

But the writer to the Hebrews also had a *Jewish background*. To the Jews, it was always dangerous to come too near to

God. 'No one', said God to Moses, 'shall see me and live' (Exodus 33:20). It was Jacob's astonished exclamation at Peniel: 'I have seen God face to face, and yet my life is preserved' (Genesis 32:30). When Manoah realized who his visitor had been, he said in terror to his wife: 'We shall surely die, for we have seen God' (Judges 13:23). The great day of Jewish worship was the Day of Atonement. That was the one day of the whole year when the high priest entered the Holy of Holies where the very presence of God was held to dwell. No one ever entered in except the high priest, and he only on that day. When he did, the law laid it down that he must not linger in the Holy Place for long 'lest he put Israel in terror'. It was dangerous to enter the presence of God; and, if anyone stayed there too long, that person might be struck dead.

In view of this, the idea of a *covenant* entered into Jewish thought. God, in his grace and in a way that was quite unmerited, approached the nation of Israel and offered them a special relationship with himself. But this unique access to God was conditional on the observance by the people of the law that he gave to them. We can see this relationship being entered into and this law being accepted in the dramatic scene in Exodus 24:3–8.

So, Israel had access to God, *but only if the people kept the law.* To break the law was sin, and sin put up a barrier which stopped the way to God. It was to take away that barrier that the system of the Levitical priesthood and sacrifices was constructed. The law was given; the people sinned; the barrier was up; the sacrifice was made; and the sacrifice was designed to open the way to God that had been closed. But the experience of life was that this was precisely what sacrifice could not do. It was proof of the ineffectiveness of the whole system that sacrifice had to go on and on and on. It was a losing and ineffective battle to remove the barrier that sin had erected between men and women and God.

The Perfect Priest and the Perfect Sacrifice

What was needed was a *perfect priest* and a *perfect sacrifice*, someone who could bring to God a sacrifice that once and for all opened the way of access to him. That, said the writer to the Hebrews, is exactly what Christ did. He is the perfect priest because he is both perfectly human and perfectly God. In his humanity, he can take us to God; and in his Godhead, he can take God to us. He has no sin. The perfect sacrifice he brings is the sacrifice of himself, a sacrifice so perfect that it never needs to be made again. To the Jews, the writer to the Hebrews said: 'All your lives, you have been looking for the perfect priest who can bring the perfect sacrifice and give you access to God. You have him in Jesus Christ and in him alone.'

To the Greeks, the writer to the Hebrews said: 'You are looking for the way from the shadows to reality; you will find it in Jesus Christ.' To the Jews, the writer to the Hebrews said: 'You are looking for that perfect sacrifice which will open the way to God which your sins have closed; you will find it in Jesus Christ.' Jesus was the one person who gave access to reality and access to God. That is the key thought of this letter.

The Riddle of the New Testament

So much is clear; but, when we turn to the other questions of introduction, Hebrews is wrapped in mystery. The New Testament scholar E. F. Scott wrote: 'The Epistle to the Hebrews is in many respects the riddle of the New Testament.' When it was written, to whom it was written, and who wrote it are questions at which we can only guess. The very history of the letter shows how its mystery is to be treated with a certain reserve and suspicion. It was a long time before it became an unquestioned New Testament book. The first list of New Testament books, the Muratorian Canon, compiled about AD 170, does not mention it at all. The great Alexandrian scholars of the second and third centuries, Clement and Origen, knew it and loved it but agreed that its place as Scripture was disputed. Of the great African fathers of the same period, Cyprian never mentions it and Tertullian knows that its place was disputed. Eusebius, the early church historian, says that it ranked among the disputed books. It was not until the time of Athanasius, in the middle of the fourth century, that Hebrews was definitely accepted as a New Testament book, and even the founder of the Reformation, Martin Luther, was not too sure about it. It is strange to think how long this great book had to wait for full recognition.

When was it Written?

The only information we have comes from the letter itself. Clearly, it is written for what we might call second-generation Christians (2:3). The story was transmitted to its recipients by those who had heard the Lord. The members of the community to whom it was written were not new to the Christian faith; they ought to have been mature (5:12). They must have had a long history, for they are called to look back on the former days (10:32). They had a great history behind them and heroic martyr figures on which they ought to look back for inspiration (13:7).

The thing that will help us most in dating the letter is its references to persecution. It is clear that at one time their leaders had died for their faith (13:7). It is clear that they themselves had not yet suffered persecution, for they had not yet resisted to the point of shedding their blood (12:4). It is also clear that they have had ill-treatment to suffer, for they have had to undergo the looting of their goods (10:32–4). And it is clear from the outlook of the letter that there is a risk of persecution about to come. From all that, it is safe to say that this letter must have been written between two persecutions, in days when Christians were not actually persecuted but were nonetheless unpopular. Now, the first persecution was in the time of Nero in the year AD 64; and the next was in the time of Domitian about AD 85. Somewhere between these dates, this letter was written – most likely nearer to Domitian's rule. If we take the date as AD 80, we shall not be far wrong.

To Whom was it Written?

Once again, we have to be dependent on such hints as we get from the letter itself. One thing is certain: it cannot have been written to any of the great churches, or the name of the place could not have so completely vanished. Let us set down what we know. The letter was written to a long-established church (5:12). It was written to a church which had at some time in the past suffered persecution (10:32–4). It was written to a church which had had great days and great teachers and leaders (13:7). It was written to a church which had not been directly founded by the apostles (2:3). It was written to a church which had been marked by generosity and liberality (6:10).

We do have one direct hint. Among the closing greetings, we find the sentence, as the Revised Standard Version translates it: 'Those who come from Italy send you greetings' (13:24). Taken by itself, that phrase could mean either that the letter was written *from* Italy or that it was written *to* Italy; but the greater likelihood is that it was written *to* Italy. Suppose I am in Glasgow and am writing to some place abroad. I would not be likely to say: 'All the people from Glasgow greet you.' I would be much more likely to say:

'All the people in Glasgow greet you.' But suppose I am somewhere abroad where there is a little colony of Glaswegians, I might well say: 'All the people from Glasgow send you their greetings.' So, we may say that the letter was written *to Italy*; and, if it was written to Italy, it was almost certainly written to Rome.

But, quite certainly, it was not written to the church at Rome as a whole. If it had been, it would not have lost its title. Furthermore, it gives the unmistakable impression that it was written to a small body of like-minded individuals. Moreover, it was obviously written to a scholarly group. From 5:12, we can see that they had been under instruction for some time and were preparing themselves to become teachers of the Christian faith. Still further, Hebrews demands such a knowledge of the Old Testament that it must always have been a book written by a scholar for scholars.

When we sum it all up, we can say that Hebrews is a letter written by a great teacher to a little group or college of Christians in Rome. He was their teacher; at the time he was separated from them and was afraid that they were drifting away from the faith; and so he wrote this letter to them. It is not so much a letter as a talk. It does not begin like Paul's letters do, although it ends with greetings as a letter does. The writer himself calls it 'a word of exhortation' (13:22).

By Whom was it Written?

Perhaps the most insoluble problem of all is the problem of its authorship. It was precisely that uncertainty which kept it so long on the fringes of the New Testament. The title in the earliest days was simply: 'To the Hebrews'. No author's name was given; no one connected it directly with the name of Paul. Clement of Alexandria used to think that Paul might have written it in Hebrew and that Luke translated it, for the style is quite different from that of Paul. Origen made a famous remark: 'who wrote the Letter to the Hebrews only God knows for certain'. Tertullian thought that Barnabas wrote it. Jerome said the Latin Church did not receive it as Paul's and, speaking of the author, said: 'the writer to the Hebrews whoever he was'. St Augustine felt the same way about it. Luther declared that Paul could never have written it because the thought was not his. The reformer John Calvin said that he could not bring himself to think that this letter was a letter of Paul.

At no time in the history of the Church did anyone ever really think that Paul wrote Hebrews. How then did it get attached to his name? It happened very simply. When the New Testament came into its final form, there was of course argument about which books were to be included and which were not. To settle it, one test was used. Was a book the work of an apostle or at least the work of one who had been in direct contact with the apostles? By this time, Hebrews was known and loved throughout the Church. Most people felt, like Origen, that God alone knew who wrote it; but they wanted it. They felt it *must* go into the New Testament, and the only way to ensure that this happened was to include it with the thirteen letters of Paul. Hebrews won its way into the New Testament on the grounds of its own greatness; but, to get in, it had to be included with the letters of Paul and come under his name. People knew quite well that it was not Paul's, but they included it among his letters because no one knew who wrote it and yet it had to go in.

The Author of Hebrews

Can we guess who the author was? Many candidates have been put forward. We can only glance at three of the many suggestions.

(1) Tertullian thought that Barnabas wrote it. Barnabas was a native of Cyprus; the people of Cyprus were famous for the excellence of the Greek they spoke; and Hebrews is written in the best Greek in the New Testament. Barnabas was a Levite (Acts 4:36) and, of all people in the New Testament, he would have had the closest knowledge of the priestly and sacrificial system on which the whole thought of the letter is based. He is called a son of *encouragement*; the Greek word is *paraklēsis*; and Hebrews calls itself a word of *paraklēsis* (13:22). He was one of the few people acceptable to both Jews and Greeks and at home in both worlds of thought. It might be that Barnabas wrote this letter; but, if so, it is strange that his name should vanish in connection with it.

(2) Luther was sure that Apollos was the author. Apollos, according to the New Testament mention of him, was a Jew, born at Alexandria, an eloquent man and well versed in the Scriptures (Acts 18:24ff.; 1 Corinthians 1:12, 3:4). The person who wrote this letter knew the Scriptures, was eloquent, and thought and argued in the way that a cultured Alexandrian would. The person who wrote Hebrews was certainly someone like Apollos in thought and in background.

(3) The most romantic of all conjectures is that of Adolf von Harnack, the great German scholar. He thought that maybe Aquila and Priscilla wrote it between them. Aquila was a teacher (Acts 18:26). Their house in Rome was a church in itself (Romans 16:5). Harnack thought that that is why the letter begins with no greetings and why the writer's name has vanished – because the main author of Hebrews was a woman, and a woman was not allowed to teach.

But, when we come to the end of conjecture, we are compelled to say, as Origen said 1,800 years ago, that only God knows who wrote Hebrews. To us, the author must remain a voice and nothing more; but we can be thankful to God for the work of this great nameless individual who wrote with incomparable skill and beauty about the Jesus who is the way to reality and the way to God.

HEBREWS

THE END OF FRAGMENTS

Hebrews 1:1–3

> It was in many parts and in many ways that God spoke
> to our fathers in the prophets in time gone past; but in
> the end of these days he has spoken to us in One who is
> a Son, a Son whom he destined to enter into posses-
> sion of all things, a Son by whose agency he made the
> universe. He was the very effulgence of God's glory;
> he was the exact expression of God's very essence. He
> bore everything onwards by the word of his power; and,
> after he had made purification for the sins of men, he
> took his royal seat at the right hand of the glory in the
> heights.

THIS is the most stylistically impressive piece of Greek in the
whole New Testament. It is a passage that any classical
Greek orator would have been proud to write. The writer of
Hebrews has brought to it every possible skill and form of
word and rhythm that the beautiful and flexible Greek
language could provide. In Greek, the two adverbs which we
have translated *in many parts* and *in many ways* are single
words, *polumerōs* and *polutropōs*. *Polu-* in such a combi-
nation means *many*, and it was a habit of the great Greek
orators, like Demosthenes, the greatest of them all, to weave

such sonorous words into the first paragraph of a speech. The writer to the Hebrews felt that, since this letter was to speak of the supreme revelation of God, the ideas must be clothed in the noblest language that it was possible to find.

There is something of interest even here. The person who wrote this letter must have been trained in Greek oratory. When he became a Christian, he did not throw his training away. *He used the talent he had in the service of Jesus Christ.* The lovely legend of the acrobatic tumbler who became a monk is familiar to many. He felt that he had so little to offer. One day, someone saw him go into the chapel and stand before the statue of the Virgin Mary. He hesitated for a moment and then began to go through his acrobatic routine. When he had completed his tumbling, he knelt in adoration; and then, says the legend, the statue of the Virgin Mary came to life, stepped down from her pedestal and gently wiped the sweat from the brow of the acrobat who had offered all he had to give. When people become Christians, they are not asked to abandon all the talents they once had; they are asked to use them in the service of Jesus Christ and of his Church.

The basic idea of this letter is that Jesus Christ alone brings to men and women the full revelation of God and that he alone enables them to enter into the very presence of God. The writer begins by contrasting Jesus with the prophets who had gone before. He talks about him coming *in the end of these days*. The Jews divided all time into two ages – the present age and the age to come. In between, they set the day of the Lord. The present age was wholly bad; the age to come was to be the golden age of God. The day of the Lord was to be like the birth-pangs of the new age. So, the writer to the Hebrews says: 'The old time is passing away; the age of incompleteness is gone; the time of guessing and feeling our way is at an end; the new age, the age of God, has dawned in

Christ.' He sees the world and human thought enter, as it were, into a new beginning with Christ. In Jesus, God has entered humanity, eternity has invaded time, and things can never be the same again.

He contrasts Jesus with the prophets, for they were always believed to be the confidants of God. Long ago, Amos had said: 'The Lord God does nothing without revealing his secret to his servants the prophets' (Amos 3:7). Philo had said: 'The prophet is the interpreter of the God who speaks within.' He had also referred to the prophets as 'interpreters of the God who uses them as instruments to reveal to men that which he wills'. In later days, this idea had been turned into a mechanical exercise. The second-century Christian writer Athenagoras spoke of God moving the mouths of the prophets as someone might play upon a musical instrument and of the Spirit breathing into them as a flute-player breathes into a flute. At about the same time, another Christian scholar, Justin Martyr, spoke of the divine coming down from heaven and sweeping across the prophets as a plectrum sweeps across a harp or a lute. In the end, the prophets were seen as having really no more to do with their message than a musical instrument had to do with the music it played or a pen with the message it wrote. That was making it all too mechanical, for even the finest musicians are to some extent at the mercy of their instruments and cannot produce great music out of a piano in which certain notes are missing or out of tune, and even the finest writers are to some extent at the mercy of their tools. God cannot reveal more than human beings can understand. His revelation comes through human minds and hearts. That is exactly what the writer to the Hebrews saw.

He says that the revelation of God which came through the prophets was *in many parts* (*polumerōs*) and *in many ways* (*polutropōs*). There are two ideas there.

(1) The revelation of the prophets had a magnificent diversity which made it a tremendous thing. From age to age, they had spoken, always fitting their message to the age, never letting it be out of date. At the same time, that revelation was *fragmentary* and had to be presented in such a way that the limitations of the time would understand. One of the most interesting things is to see how, time after time, the prophets are characterized by one idea. For instance, Amos is '*a cry for social justice*'. Isaiah had grasped the *holiness of God*. Hosea, because of his own bitter home experience, had realized the wonder of the *forgiving love of God*. Out of their own experience of life and out of the experience of Israel, the prophets had each grasped and expressed a *fragment* of the truth of God. None had grasped the fullness of truth in its entirety; but with Jesus it was different. He was not a fragment of the truth; he was the whole truth. In him, God displayed not some part of himself but all of himself.

(2) The prophets used many methods. They used the method of *speech*. When speech failed, they used the method of *dramatic action* (cf. 1 Kings 11:29–32; Jeremiah 13:1–9, 27:1–7; Ezekiel 4:1–3, 5:1–4). The prophets had to use human methods to transmit their own part of the truth of God. Again, it was different with Jesus. He revealed God *by being himself.* It is not so much what he said and did that shows us what God is like; it is what he was.

The revelation of the prophets was great and came in many forms, but it was fragmentary and presented by such methods as they could find to make it effective. The revelation of God in Jesus was complete and was presented in Jesus himself. In a word, the prophets were the *friends* of God; but Jesus was the *Son*. The prophets grasped *part* of the mind of God; but Jesus *was* that mind. It is to be noted that it is no part of the purpose of the writer to the Hebrews to belittle the prophets;

it is his aim to establish the supremacy of Jesus Christ. He is
not saying that there is a *break* between the Old Testament
revelation and that of the New Testament; he is stressing the
fact that there is *continuity*, but continuity that ends in
consummation.

The writer to the Hebrews uses two great pictures to
describe what Jesus was. He says that he was the *apaugasma*
of God's glory. *Apaugasma* can mean one of two things in
Greek. It can mean *brilliance*, the light which shines out, or
it can mean *reflection*, the light which is reflected. Here, it
probably means *brilliance*. Jesus is the shining of God's glory
among us.

He says that he was the *character* of God's very essence.
In Greek, *character* means two things – first, a *seal*, and,
second, the *impression* that the seal leaves on the wax. The
impression has the exact form of the seal. So, when the writer
to the Hebrews said that Jesus was the *character* of the being
of God, he meant that he was the exact image of God. Just as,
when you look at the impression, you see exactly what the
seal which made it is like, so when you look at Jesus you see
exactly what God is like.

In his commentary, the nineteenth-century scholar and
churchman C. J. Vaughan has pointed out that this passage
tells us six great things about Jesus.

(1) The original glory of God belongs to him. Here is a
wonderful thought. Jesus is God's glory; therefore, we see
with amazing clarity that the glory of God consists not in
crushing men and women and reducing them to miserable
submission and slavery, but in serving them and loving them
and in the end dying for them. It is not the glory of shattering
power but the glory of suffering love.

(2) The destined empire belongs to Jesus. The New
Testament writers never doubted his ultimate triumph. Think

of it. They were thinking of a Galilaean carpenter who was crucified as a criminal on a cross on a hill outside the city of Jerusalem. They themselves faced savage persecution and were the humblest of people. As the Yorkshire poet Sir William Watson said of them:

> So to the wild wolf Hate were sacrificed
> The panting, huddled flock, whose crime was Christ.

And yet they never doubted the eventual victory. They were quite certain that God's love was backed by his power and that in the end the kingdoms of the world would be the kingdoms of the Lord and of his Christ.

(3) The creative action belongs to Jesus. The early Church held that the Son had been God's agent in creation, that in some way God had originally created the world through him. They were filled with the thought that the one who had created the world would also be the one who redeemed it.

(4) The sustaining power belongs to Jesus. These early Christians had a tremendous grip of the doctrine of *providence*. They did not think of God as creating the world and then leaving it to itself. Somehow and somewhere, they saw a power that was carrying the world and each life on to a destined end. They believed, as Tennyson wrote in *In Memoriam*:

> That nothing walks with aimless feet;
> That not one life shall be destroy'd,
> Or cast as rubbish to the void,
> When God hath made the pile complete.

(5) To Jesus belongs the redemptive work. By his sacrifice, he paid the price of sin; by his continual presence, he liberates from sin.

(6) To Jesus belongs the exaltation as mediator. He has taken his place on the right hand of glory; but the tremendous thought of the writer to the Hebrews is that he is there not as our judge but as one who makes intercession for us, so that, when we enter into the presence of God, we go not to hear his justice prosecute us but to hear his love plead for us.

ABOVE THE ANGELS

Hebrews 1:4–14

He was the superior to the angels, in proportion as he had received a more excellent rank than they. For to which of the angels did God ever say: 'It is my *Son* that you are; it is I who this day have begotten you'? And again: 'I will be to him a Father, and he will be to me a Son.' And again, when he brings his honoured one into the world of men, he says: 'And let all the angels of God bow down before him.' As for the angels, he says: 'He who makes his angels winds and his servants a flame of fire.' But, as for the Son, he says: 'God is your throne forever and forever, and the sceptre of righteousness is the sceptre of your kingdom. You have loved justice and hated lawlessness; therefore God has anointed you, even your God, with the oil of exultation above your fellows.' And, 'You in the beginning, O Lord, laid the foundations of the earth, and the heavens are the work of your hands. They shall perish but you remain unalterable. All of them will grow old like a garment, and like a mantle you will fold them up and they will be changed. But you are ever yourself, and your years will not fail.' To which of the angels did he ever say: 'Sit at my right hand till I make your enemies your footstool'? Are they not all ministering spirits,

continually being despatched on service, for the sake
of those who are destined to enter into possession of
salvation?

In the previous passage, the writer was concerned to prove
the superiority of Jesus over all the prophets. Now he is
concerned to prove his superiority over the angels. That he
thinks it worth while to do this proves the place that belief in
angels had in the thought of the Jews of his day. At this time,
such a belief was on the increase. The reason was that
people were more and more impressed with what is called
the transcendence of God. They felt more and more the
distance and the difference between God and themselves. The
result was that they came to think of the angels as inter-
mediaries between God and human beings. They came to
believe that the angels bridged the gulf between God and
men and women; that God spoke to them through the angels
and the angels carried their prayers into the presence of God.
We see this process particularly in one instance. In the Old
Testament, the law was given directly by God to Moses,
without the need of an intermediary. But, in New Testament
times, the Jews believed that God gave the law first to angels
who then passed it on to Moses, direct communication
between human beings and God being unthinkable (cf. Acts
7:53; Galatians 3:19).

If we look at some of the basic Jewish beliefs about angels,
we will see those beliefs reappearing in this passage. God
lived surrounded by his angelic hosts (Isaiah 6; 1 Kings
22:19). Sometimes the angels are thought of as God's army
(Joshua 5:14f.). In Greek, the word for *angels* is *aggeloi*, and
in Hebrew it is *mal'akim*. In both languages, the meaning is
messenger as well as *angel*. In fact, *messenger* is the more
common meaning. The angels were really the beings who
were the instruments in the bringing of God's word and the

working of God's will in the world. They were said to be made of an ethereal fiery substance like blazing light. They were created on either the second or the fifth day of creation. They did not eat or drink, and they did not have children. Sometimes they were believed to be immortal, although they could be annihilated by God; but there was another belief about their existence, as we shall see. Some of them, the seraphim, the cherubim and the ofanim (-*im* is the plural ending of Hebrew nouns), were always around the throne of God. They were thought of as having more knowledge than human beings, especially of the future; but they did not possess that knowledge by right but rather because of 'what they had heard behind the curtain'. They were thought of as the kind of entourage, the *familia*, of God. They were thought of as God's senate; God did nothing without consulting them. For instance, when God said: 'Let *us* make humankind' (Genesis 1:26), it was to the angel senate that he was speaking. Often, the angels remonstrated with God and laid objections to his purposes. In particular, they objected to the creation of human life, and at that time many of them were annihilated; and they objected to the giving of the law and attacked Moses on his way up Mount Sinai. This was because they were jealous and did not want to share their position or privileges with any other creature.

There were millions and millions of angels. It was not until quite late that the Jews assigned names to them. There were, in particular, the seven angels of the presence, who were the archangels. Of these, the principal ones were Raphael, Uriel, Phanuel, Gabriel, the angel who brought God's messages to his people, and Michael, the angel who presided over the destinies of Israel. The angels had many duties. They brought God's messages to individuals. In that case, they delivered their message and vanished (Judges 13:20). They intervened for God in the events of history (2 Kings 19:35–6). There were 200 angels who controlled the movements of the stars and kept them in their courses. There was an angel who controlled the never-ending succession of the years and months and days. There was an angel, a mighty prince, who was over the sea. There were angels of the frost, the dew, the rain, the snow, the hail, the thunder and the lightning. There were angels who were wardens of hell and torturers of the damned. There were recording angels who wrote down every single word which everyone spoke. There were destroying angels and angels of punishment. There was Satan, the prosecuting angel, who on every day except the Day of Atonement continuously brought charges against men and women before God. There was the angel of death who went out only at God's bidding and who impartially delivered his summons to good and to evil people alike. Every nation had its guardian angel who had the *prostasia*, the presidency over it. Every individual had a guardian angel. Even little children had their angels (Matthew 18:10). So many were the angels that the Rabbis could even say: 'Every blade of grass has its angel.'

There was one special belief, held only by some, which is indirectly referred to in the passage that we are studying. The common belief was that the angels were immortal; but there were some who believed that they lived for only one day. There was a belief in some Rabbinic schools that 'every day God creates a new company of angels who utter a song before him and are gone'. 'The angels are renewed every morning and after they have praised God they return to the stream of fire from whence they came.' Second Esdras [4 Ezra] 8:21 speaks of the God 'before whom the hosts of angels stand trembling and at whose command they are changed to wind and fire'. A Rabbinic homily makes one of the angels say:

'God changes us every hour . . . Sometimes he makes us fire, at other times wind.' That is what the writer to the Hebrews means when he talks of God making his angels wind and fire.

With this vast angelology, many believed there was a very real danger that the angels would come to intervene between God and them. It was necessary to show that the Son was far greater than the angels and that those who knew the Son needed no angel to be their intermediary with God. The writer to the Hebrews does it by choosing what are for him a series of proof texts in which the Son is given a higher place than was ever given to any angel. The texts he quotes are: Psalm 2:7; 2 Samuel 7:14; Psalm 97:7 or Deuteronomy 32:43; Psalm 104:4; Psalm 45:7–8; Psalm 102:26–7; Psalm 110:1. Some of these texts differ from the versions we know because the writer to the Hebrews was quoting from the Septuagint, the Greek version of the Old Testament, which is not always the same as the original Hebrew from which our versions are translated. Some of the proof texts he chooses seem very strange. For instance, 2 Samuel 7:14 is, in the original, a simple reference to Solomon and has nothing to do with the Son or the Messiah. Psalm 102:26–7 is a reference to God and not to the Son. But whenever the early Christians found a text with the word *son* or the word *Lord*, they considered themselves quite entitled to take it out of its context and to apply it to Jesus.

There was one danger which the writer to the Hebrews wished at all costs to avoid. The doctrine of angels is a lovely thing; but it has one danger. It introduces a series of beings other than Jesus through whom men and women make their approach to God. In Christianity, there is no need for anyone else in between. Because of Jesus and what he did, we have direct access to God. As Tennyson in 'The Higher Pantheism' had it:

> Speak to him thou for he hears, and Spirit
>   with spirit can meet –
> Closer is he than breathing, and nearer
>   than hands and feet.

The writer to the Hebrews lays down the great truth that we need neither human nor supernatural beings to bring us into the presence of God. Jesus Christ has broken every barrier down and opened a direct way for us to God.

THE SALVATION WE DARE NOT NEGLECT

Hebrews 2:1–4

> We must, therefore, with very special intensity pay attention to the things that we have heard. For, if the word which was spoken through the medium of the angels proved itself to be certified as valid, and if every transgression and disobedience of it received its just recompense, how shall we escape if we neglect so great a salvation, a salvation of such a kind that it had its origin in the words of the Lord, and was then guaranteed to us by those who had heard it from his lips, while God himself added his own witness to it by signs and wonders and manifold deeds of power, and by giving us each a share of the Holy Spirit, according as he willed it?

THE writer is arguing from the less to the greater. He has in his mind two revelations. One was the revelation of the law which came *by the medium of the angels*, that is to say, the Ten Commandments. Now, any breach of that law was followed by strict and just punishment. The other was the revelation which came *through the medium of Jesus Christ, the Son*. Because it came in and through the Son, it was infinitely greater than the revelation of God's truth brought by the angels; and therefore any transgression of it must be followed by a far more terrible punishment. If people cannot ignore the revelation which came *through the angels*, how much less can they ignore the revelation which came *through the Son*?

In the first verse, there may be an even more vivid picture than there is in the translation which we have used. The two key words are *prosechein* and *pararrein*. We have taken *prosechein* to mean *to pay attention to*, which is one of its most common meanings. *Pararrein* is a word of many meanings. It is used of something flowing or slipping past; it can be used of a ring that has slipped off the finger, of a particle of food that has slipped down the wrong way, of a topic that has slipped into the conversation, of a point which has escaped someone in the course of an argument, of some fact that has slipped out of the mind, of something that has ebbed or leaked away. It is regularly used of something which has carelessly or thoughtlessly been allowed to become lost.

But both these words also have a nautical sense. *Prosechein* can mean *to moor a ship*; and *pararrein* can be used of a ship which has been carelessly allowed to slip past a harbour or a haven because the captain has forgotten to allow for the wind or the current or the tide. So, this first verse could be very vividly translated: 'Therefore, we must the more eagerly anchor our lives to the things that we have been taught in case the ship of life should drift past the harbour and be wrecked.' It is a vivid picture of a ship drifting to destruction because the pilot is asleep.

For most of us, the threat of life is not so much that we should plunge into disaster but that we should drift into sin. There are few people who, deliberately and in a moment, turn their backs on God; there are many who day by day drift

further and further away from him. There are not many who
in one moment of time commit some disastrous sin; there
are many who almost imperceptibly involve themselves in
some situation and suddenly awake to find that they have
ruined life for themselves and broken someone else's heart.
We must be continually on the alert against the peril of drifting
in life.

The writer to the Hebrews characterizes under two
headings the sins for which the law brings its punishment: he
calls them *transgression* and *disobedience*. The first of these
words is *parabasis*, which literally means *the stepping across
a line*. There is a line drawn both by knowledge and by conscience, and to step across it is sin. The second is *parakoē*.
Parakoē begins by meaning *imperfect hearing*, as, for
instance, of someone who is deaf. Then it goes on to mean
careless hearing, the kind which through inattention either
misunderstands or fails to catch what has been said. It ends
by meaning *unwillingness to hear*, and therefore *disobedience
to the voice of God*. It is the deliberate shutting of the ears to
the commands and warnings and invitations of God.

The writer to the Hebrews ends this paragraph by stating
three ways in which the Christian revelation is unique.

(1) It is unique in its *origin*. It came direct from Jesus
himself. It does not consist of guessing and feeling our way
towards God; it is the very voice of God himself which comes
to us in Jesus Christ.

(2) It is unique in its *transmission*. It came to the people
to whom Hebrews was written from those who had
themselves heard it direct from the lips of Jesus. The person
who can pass on the Christian truth to others is the one who
knows Christ 'other than at second hand'. We can never teach
what we do not know; and we can teach others of Christ only
when we know him ourselves.

(3) It is unique in its *effectiveness*. It produced signs and wonders and deeds of power of many kinds. Someone once congratulated the nineteenth-century preacher Thomas Chalmers after one of his great speeches. 'Yes,' he said, 'but *what did it do?*' As the theologian James Denney used to say, the ultimate object of Christianity is to make bad people good; and the proof of real Christianity is the fact that it can change the lives of individuals. The moral miracles of Christianity are still plain for all to see.

THE RECOVERY OF OUR LOST DESTINY

Hebrews 2:5–9

> It was not to angels that he subjected the order of things to come of which we are speaking. Somewhere in Scripture, someone bears this witness to that fact: 'What is man that you remember him? Or the son of man that you visit him? For a little time, you made him lower than the angels; you crowned him with glory and honour; you set him over the work of your hands; you subjected all things beneath his feet.' The fact that all things have been subjected to him means that nothing has been left unsubjected to him. But, as things are, we see that all things are not in a state of subjection to him. But we do see him who was for a little while made lower than the angels, Jesus himself, crowned with glory and honour because of the suffering of his death, a suffering which came to him in order that, by the grace of God, he might drain the cup of death for every man.

IT is by no means an easy task to grasp the meaning of this passage; but, when we do, it is a tremendous thing. The writer begins with a quotation from Psalm 8:4–6. If we are ever to understand this passage correctly, we must understand one thing: *the whole reference of Psalm 8 is to human beings*. It sings of the glory that God gave to *men and women*. There is no reference to the Messiah.

There is a phrase in the psalm which makes it difficult for us to grasp that. The phrase is literally translated as *the son of man*. We are so used to hearing that phrase applied to Jesus that we tend always to take it to refer to him. But, in Hebrew, *a son of man* always means simply *a man*. We find, for instance, that, in the Revised Standard Version, in the book of the prophet Ezekiel, more than eighty times God addresses Ezekiel as *son of man*. 'Son of man, set your face toward Jerusalem' (Ezekiel 21:2). 'Son of man, prophesy, and say . . .' (Ezekiel 30:2).

In the psalm quoted here, the two parallel phrases which we have translated as 'What is man that you remember him?' and 'Or the son of man that you visit him?' are different ways of saying exactly the same thing. The psalm is a great lyric cry of the glory of human life as God meant it to be. It is, in fact, an expansion of the great promise of God at creation in Genesis 1:28, when he said to Adam: 'Have dominion over the fish of the sea and over the birds of the air and over every living thing that moves upon the earth.'

The glory of human beings, incidentally, is even greater than the Authorized Version would lead us to understand. It tells us that God has made them 'a little lower than the angels' (Psalm 8:5). That is a correct translation of the *Greek* but not of the *original Hebrew*. In the original Hebrew, it is said that they are made a little lower than the *Elohim*; and *Elohim* is the regular word for *God*. What the psalmist really wrote was that human beings had been made 'little less than God', which, in fact, is the translation of the Revised Standard Version. So, this psalm sings of the glory of human

28

beings, who were made little less than divine and whom God meant to have dominion over everything in the world.

But, the writer to the Hebrews goes on, the situation with which we are confronted is very different. Men and women were meant to have dominion over everything – *but they have not*. They are creatures who are frustrated by their circumstances, defeated by their temptations and surrounded by their own weaknesses. The ones who should be free are bound; the ones who should be rulers are slaves. As the writer G. K. Chesterton said, whatever else is or is not true, this one thing is certain: we are not what we were meant to be.

The writer to the Hebrews goes further. Into this situation came Jesus Christ. He suffered and he died; and, because he suffered and died, he entered into glory. And that suffering and death and glory are all for us, because he died to make us what we ought to be. He died to rid us of our frustration and our bondage and our weakness and to give us the dominion we ought to have. He died to re-create us until we become what we were originally created to be.

In this passage, there are three basic ideas. (1) God created men and women only a little less than himself, to have control over all things. (2) Through their sin, they entered into defeat instead of control. (3) Into this state of defeat came Jesus Christ in order that by his life and death and glory he might make men and women what they were meant to be.

We may put it another way. The writer to the Hebrews shows us three things. (1) He shows us *the ideal of what we should be* – kin to God and rulers of the universe. (2) He shows us *the actual human condition* – the frustration instead of the control, the failure instead of the glory. (3) He shows us *how the actual can be changed into the ideal through Christ*. The writer to the Hebrews sees in Christ the one who by his sufferings and his glory can make us what we were meant to be and what, without him, we could never be.

THE ESSENTIAL SUFFERING

Hebrews 2:10–18

> For, in his work of bringing many sons to glory, it was fitting that he for whom everything exists and through whom everything exists should make the pioneer of salvation fully adequate for his destined work through suffering. For he who sanctifies and they who are sanctified must come of one stock. It is for this reason that he does not hesitate to call them brothers, as when he says: 'I will tell your name to my brothers; I will sing hymns to you in the midst of the gathering of your people.' And again: 'I will put all my trust in him.' And again: 'Behold me and the children whom God gave to me.' The children then have a common flesh and blood and he completely shared in them, so that, by that death of his, he might bring to nothing him who has the power of death, and might set free all those who, for fear of death, were all their lives liable to a slave's existence. For I presume that it is not angels that he helps; but it is the seed of Abraham that he helps. So he had in all things to be made like his brothers, so that he might become a merciful and faithful high priest in the things which pertain to God, to win forgiveness for the sins of his people. For in that he himself was tried and suffered, he is able to help those who are undergoing trial.

HERE, the writer to the Hebrews uses one of the great titles of Jesus. He calls him *the pioneer (archēgos) of glory*. The same word is used of Jesus in Acts 3:15, 5:31; Hebrews 12:2. At its simplest, it means *head* or *chief*. So, Zeus is the *head* of the gods and a general is the *head* of his army. It can mean a *founder* or *originator*. So, it is used of the founder of a city or of a family or of a philosophic school. It can be used in the sense of *source* or *origin*. So, a good governor is said to be the *archēgos* of peace and a bad governor the *archēgos* of confusion.

One basic idea clings to the word in all its uses. An *archēgos* is someone who begins something in order that others may enter into it. The word is used to describe the person who begins a family so that some day others may be born into it, who founds a city in order that others may some day live in it, who founds a philosophic school so that others may follow into the truth and the peace that that person has already discovered; someone who is the author of blessings into which others may also enter. An *archēgos* is the one who blazes a trail for others to follow. Let us take an analogy. Suppose a ship is on the rocks, and the only way to safety is for someone to swim ashore with a line so that, once the line is secured, others might follow. The one who is first to swim ashore will be the *archēgos* of the safety of the others. This is what the writer to the Hebrews means when he says that Jesus is the *archēgos* of our salvation. Jesus has blazed the trail to God for us to follow.

How was Jesus enabled to take on this role? The Authorized and Revised Standard Versions say that God made him *perfect* through suffering. The verb translated as *make perfect* is *teleioun*, which comes from the adjective *teleios*, which is usually translated as *perfect*. But, in the New Testament, *teleios* has a very special meaning. It has nothing to do with abstract, metaphysical and philosophic perfection. It is used, for instance, of an animal which is unblemished and fit to be offered as a sacrifice; of a scholar who is no longer at the elementary stage but is mature; of a human being or an animal who is fully grown; of a Christian who is no longer on the fringe of the Church but who is baptized. The basic meaning of *teleios* in the New Testament is always that the thing or person described in this way *fully carries out the purpose for which he or she is designed*. Therefore, the verb *teleioun* will mean not so much *to make perfect* as *to make fully adequate for the task for which designed*. So, what the writer to the Hebrews is saying is that, through suffering, Jesus was made fully able to complete the task of being the pioneer of our salvation.

Why should that be?

(1) It was through his sufferings that he was really *identified* with us. The writer to the Hebrews quotes three Old Testament texts as forecasts of this identity with men and women – Psalm 22:22; Isaiah 8:17, 8:18. If Jesus had come into this world in a form in which he could never have suffered, he would have been quite different from us and so no Saviour for us. As Jeremy Taylor, the seventeenth-century churchman, said: 'When God would save men, he did it by way of a man.' It is, in fact, this identification with us which is the essence of the Christian idea of God. When the Greeks thought of their gods, they thought of them as Tennyson pictures them in 'The Song of the Lotos-Eaters':

> For they lie beside their nectar, and the bolts are
>   hurl'd
> Far below them in the valleys, and the clouds are
>   lightly curl'd
> Round their golden houses, girdled with the
>   gleaming world:
> Where they smile in secret, looking over wasted
>   lands,
> Blight and famine, plague and earthquake,
>   roaring deeps and fiery sands,

Clanging fights, and flaming towns, and sinking
  ships, and praying hands.

The basis of the Greek idea of God was *detachment*; the basis
of the Christian idea is *identity*. Through his sufferings, Jesus
Christ identified himself with us.

(2) Through this identity, Jesus Christ *sympathizes* with
us. He literally *feels* with us. It is almost impossible to understand another person's sorrows and sufferings unless we have
been through them. A person without a trace of nerves has no
conception of the tortures of nervousness. A person who is
perfectly physically fit has no conception of the weariness of
the person who is easily tired or the suffering of the person
who is never free from pain. A person who learns easily often
cannot understand why someone who is slow finds things so
difficult. A person who has never known sorrow cannot
understand the pain at the heart of the person into whose life
grief has come. A person who has never loved can never
understand either the sudden glory or the aching loneliness
in the lover's heart. Before we can have sympathy, we must
go through the same things that the other person has gone
through – and that is precisely what Jesus did.

(3) Because he sympathizes, Jesus can really *help*. He has
met our sorrows; he has faced our temptations. As a result,
he knows exactly what help we need; and he can give it.

GREATER THAN THE GREATEST

Hebrews 3:1–6

> Brothers who are dedicated to God, you who are sharers
> in heaven's calling, because of all this you must fix your
> attention on him whom our creed holds to be the apostle
> and the high priest of God, I mean Jesus, for he was

faithful to him who appointed him, just as Moses was in all his house. For he was deemed worthy of more honour than Moses, in so far as the man who builds and equips the house has more honour than the house itself. For every house is built and equipped by someone; but it is God who builds and equips all things. Moses was faithful in all his house, but his role was the role of a servant, and his purpose was to bear witness to the things which some day would be spoken. But Christ is over his house because he is a Son. We are his house if only we keep strong the confidence and pride of our hope to the end.

LET us remember the conviction with which the writer to the Hebrews starts. The basis of his thought is that the supreme revelation of God comes through Jesus Christ and that only through him can individuals have real access to God. He began by proving that Jesus was superior to the prophets; he went on to prove that Jesus was superior to the angels; and now he proceeds to prove that Jesus is superior to Moses.

It might at first sight seem that this is an anticlimax. But it was not so for a Jew. For the Jews, Moses held a place which was utterly unique. He was the man with whom God had spoken face to face as with his friend. He was the direct recipient of the Ten Commandments, the very law of God. The greatest thing in all the world for the Jews was the law, and Moses and the law were one and the same thing. In the second century, a Jewish teacher called Rabbi Jose ben Chalafta, commenting on this very passage which declared that Moses was faithful in all his house, said: 'God calls Moses faithful in all his house, and thereby he ranked him higher than the ministering angels themselves.' For a Jew, the step that the writer to the Hebrews takes is the logical and inevitable step in the argument. He has proved that Jesus is greater than the angels; now he must prove that he is greater than Moses, who was greater than the angels.

In fact, this quotation, which is used to tell of the greatness of Moses, is proof of the unique position which the Jews assigned to him. 'Moses was faithful in all his house.' The quotation is from Numbers 12:7. Now, the point of the argument in Numbers is that Moses differs from all the prophets. To them, God makes himself known in a vision; to Moses, he speaks 'mouth to mouth'. To the Jews, it would have been impossible to conceive that anyone ever stood closer to God than Moses did, and yet that is precisely what the writer of the Hebrews sets out to prove.

He tells his hearers *to fix their attention* on Jesus. The word he uses (*katanoein*) is significant and full of meaning. It does not mean simply to look at or to notice a thing. Anyone can look at a thing or even notice it without really seeing it. The word means to fix the attention on something in such a way that its inner meaning, the lesson that it is designed to teach, may be learned. In Luke 12:24, Jesus uses the same word when he says: '*Consider* the ravens.' He does not merely mean: '*Look* at the ravens.' He means: 'Look at the ravens and *understand and learn* the lesson that God is seeking to teach you through them.' If we are ever to learn Christian truth, a detached glance is never enough; there must be a concentrated gaze in which we focus the mind in a determined effort to see its meaning for us.

In a sense, the reason for that is implicit when the writer addresses his friends as *sharers in heaven's calling*. The call that comes to Christians has a double direction. It is a calling *from* heaven and it is a calling *to* heaven. It is a voice which comes *from* God and calls us *to* God. It is a call which demands concentrated attention because of both its origin and its destination. No one can afford merely to glance without interest at an invitation *to* God *from* God.

When we fix our attention on Jesus, what do we see? We see two things.

(1) We see the great *apostle*. No one else in the New Testament ever calls Jesus an *apostle*. That the writer to the Hebrews does so deliberately is quite clear, because *apostle* is a title he never gives to any individual. He keeps it for Christ.

What does he mean when he uses it in this way? The word *apostolos* literally means *one who is sent forth*. In Jewish terminology, it was used to describe the envoys of the Sanhedrin, the supreme court of the Jews. The Sanhedrin sent out *apostoloi* who were clothed with its authority and the bearers of its commands. In the Greek world, it frequently meant *ambassador*. So, Jesus is the supreme ambassador of God – and ambassadors have two supremely important and relevant characteristics.

(a) Ambassadors carry all the authority of the one who sends them. On one occasion, the king of Syria, Antiochus Epiphanes, invaded Egypt. Rome wanted to stop him and sent an envoy called Popillius to tell him to abandon his projected invasion. Popillius caught up with Antiochus on the borders of Egypt, and they talked of this and that, for they had known each other in Rome. Popillius did not have an army with him, not even a guard. Finally, Antiochus asked him why he had come. Quietly, Popillius told him that he had come to tell him that Rome wanted him to abandon the invasion and go home. 'I will consider it,' said Antiochus. Popillius smiled a little grimly; he took his staff and drew a circle in the earth round Antiochus. 'Consider it,' he said, 'and come to your decision before you leave that circle.' Antiochus thought for a few seconds and then said: 'Very well. I will go home.' Popillius himself had not the slightest force available – but behind him was all the power of Rome. So, Jesus came from God, and all God's grace and mercy and love and power were in his *apostolos*.

(b) The voice with which ambassadors speak is the voice of the individual or country that sent them. In a foreign land, the British ambassador's voice is the voice of Britain, and the American ambassador speaks with the voice of the United States. So, Jesus came with the voice of God; in him, God speaks.

(2) Jesus is the great *high priest*. What does that mean? This is an idea to which the writer to the Hebrews returns again and again. For now, we set down only the fundamental basis of what he means. The Latin for a priest is *pontifex*, which means a *bridge-builder*. The priest is the person who builds a bridge between men and women and God. To do that, the priest must know both human nature and God, and must be able to speak to God for men and women and in turn to speak to them for God. Jesus is the perfect high priest because he is perfectly human and perfectly God; he can represent us to God and God to us. He is the one person through whom we come to God and God comes to us.

Wherein does the superiority of Jesus over Moses lie? The picture in the mind of the writer to the Hebrews is this. He thinks of the world as God's house and God's family. We use the word *house* in a double sense. We use it in the sense of a building and also in the sense of a family. The Greeks used *oikos* in the same double sense. The world is God's house, and we are God's family. But he has already shown us the picture of Jesus as the creator of God's universe. Now, Moses was only part of God's universe, part of the house. But Jesus is the creator of the house, and the creator is bound to stand above the house itself. Moses did not create the law; he only passed it on to the people. Moses did not create the house; he only served in it. Moses did not speak of himself; all that he ever said was only a pointer to the greater things that Jesus Christ would some day say. In short, Moses was the *servant*; but Jesus was the *Son*. Moses knew a little *about* God; Jesus *was* God. Therein lies the secret of his superiority.

Now, the writer to the Hebrews uses another picture. True, the whole world is God's house; but in a special sense the Church is God's house, for in a special sense God brought it into being. That is a picture the New Testament loves (cf. 1 Peter 4:17; 1 Timothy 3:15; and especially 1 Peter 2:5). That building of the Church will stand and be indestructible only when every stone is firm; that is to say, when every member is strong in the proud and confident hope that he or she has in Jesus Christ. Each one of us is like a stone in the Church; if one stone is weak, the whole structure is endangered. The Church stands firm only when each living stone in it is rooted and grounded in faith in Jesus Christ.

WHILE TODAY STILL LASTS

Hebrews 3:7–19

> So then, as the Holy Spirit says, 'If today you will hear my voice, do not harden your hearts, as in the Provocation, as happened on the day of the Temptation in the wilderness, where your fathers tried to test me, and, in consequence, experienced for forty years what I could do. So my anger was kindled against that generation, and I said: "Always they wander in their hearts; they do not know my ways." So I swore in my anger: "Very certainly they shall not enter into my rest."' Have a care, brothers, lest that evil and disobedient heart be in any of you in a state of rebellion

against the living God. But keep on exhorting each other day by day, so long as the term 'today' can be used, lest any among you be hardened in heart by the seductiveness of sin; for you have become participators in Christ, if indeed you hold fast the beginning of your confidence firm to the end. While it is still possible to hear it being said, 'If *today* you will hear my voice,' do not harden your hearts as at the Provocation. For who heard and provoked God? Was it not all who came forth from Egypt under the leadership of Moses? Against whom was God's anger kindled for forty years? Was it not against those who had sinned and whose bones lay in the desert? To whom did he swear that they should not enter into his rest, if not to those who were disobedient? Thus we see that it was through disobedience that they could not enter in.

THE writer to the Hebrews has just been attempting to prove the unique supremacy of Jesus, and now he replaces argument with exhortation. He presses upon his hearers the inevitable consequence of this unique supremacy. If Jesus is so uniquely great, it follows that complete trust and complete obedience must be given to him. If they harden their hearts and refuse to give him their obedient trust, the consequences are bound to be terrible.

The way in which he supports his argument is very difficult for us to understand because it contains two specific allusions. He begins by quoting from Psalm 95:7–11. That Psalm appeals to those who hear it not to be like the children of Israel but, as the Authorized Version renders it, to 'Harden not your hearts, as in *the provocation*, in *the day of temptation*.' Now, the two phrases *the provocation* and *the day of temptation* translate two Hebrew words which are *place names* – Massah and Meribah. The whole is a reference to the story told in Exodus 17:1–7 and Numbers 20:1–13. These passages tell of a rebellious incident in the pilgrimage of the children of Israel. They were thirsty in the desert and turned on Moses, expressing their regret that they had ever left Egypt and renouncing their trust in God. In the Numbers version of the story, God told Moses to speak to the limestone rock, and water would gush forth. But Moses in his anger did not *speak* to the rock; he *struck* it. The water came forth; but, for this act of distrust and disobedience, God declared that Moses would never be allowed to lead the people into the promised land. 'Very certainly they shall not enter into *my rest*' means: 'Very certainly they will not enter into *the promised land*.' To wanderers in the desert, the promised land was the place of rest, and it was often called *the rest* (cf. Deuteronomy 12:9). The point is that the disobedience and the distrust of Israel cut them off from the blessings of God that they might have enjoyed.

The writer to the Hebrews says to his people: 'Beware that you do not show the same disobedience and distrust of God that your ancestors showed, and that you do not for that reason lose the blessings you might have had, just as they lost theirs.' In effect, he says: 'While there is still time, while you can still speak of "today", give God the trust and the obedience that he must have.' For the individual, 'today' means 'while life lasts', and the writer to the Hebrews is saying: 'While you have the chance, give God the submission you ought to give. Give it to him before your day closes.' There are certain great warnings here,

(1) God makes men and women an offer. Just as he offered the Israelites the blessings of the promised land, he offers to everyone the blessings of a life which is far beyond the life that can be lived without him.

(2) But, to obtain the blessings of God, two things are necessary. (a) *Trust* is necessary. We must believe that what

God says is true. We must be willing to stake our lives on his promises. (b) *Obedience* is necessary. It is just as if a doctor were to say to us: 'I can cure you if you obey my instructions implicitly.' It is just as if a teacher were to say: 'I can make you a scholar if you follow my curriculum exactly.' It is just as if a trainer were to say to an athlete: 'I can make you a champion if you do not deviate from the discipline that I lay down.' In any area of life, success depends on obedience to the word of the expert. God, if we may put it so, is the expert in life, and real happiness depends on obedience to him.

(3) To the offer of God, there is a limit. That limit is the duration of life. We never know when that limit will be reached. We speak easily about 'tomorrow'; but, for us, tomorrow may never come. All we have is today. It has been said: 'We should live each day as if it were a lifetime.' God's offer must be accepted today; the trust and the obedience must be given today – for we cannot be sure that there will be a tomorrow for us.

Here we have the supreme offer of God; but it is only for perfect trust and full obedience, and it must be accepted now – or it may be too late.

THE REST WE DARE NOT MISS

Hebrews 4:1–10

> It is true that the promise which offers entry into the rest of God still remains for us; but beware lest any of you be adjudged to have missed it. It is indeed true that we have had the good news preached to us, just as those of old had. But the word which they heard was no good to them, because it did not become woven into the very

fibre of their being through faith. It is we who have
made the decision of faith who are entering into the
rest, for of them God said: 'I swore in my anger: "Very
certainly they shall not enter into my rest."' This he
said although his works had been finished after the
foundation of the world. For somewhere in Scripture it
speaks thus about the seventh day: 'And God rested on
the seventh day from all his labours.' And it says in the
same place: 'Very certainly they shall not enter into my
rest.' Since then it remains that some people must enter
into it and since those who in former times had the
gospel preached to them did not enter because of their
lack of trust, he again defines a day, when in David,
after so long a lapse of time, he says: 'Today,' just as
he had said before: 'today if you will hear my voice do
not harden your hearts'. If Joshua had actually brought
them into rest, God would not then after that be speaking
about another day. So a Sabbath rest remains for the
people of God. He who has entered into this rest has
rest from all his works, just as God rested from his
works.

In a complicated passage like this, it is better to try to grasp
the broad lines of the thought before we look at any of the
details. The writer is really using the word *rest* (*katapausis*)
in three different senses. (1) He is using it as we would use
the peace of God. It is the greatest thing in the world to
enter into the peace of God. (2) He is using it, as he used it
in 3:12, to mean *the promised land*. To the children of Israel
who had wandered so long in the desert, the promised land
was indeed the rest of God. (3) He is using it of *the rest of
God* after the sixth day of creation, when all God's work
was completed. This way of using a word in two or three
different ways, of teasing at it until the last drop of meaning
was extracted from it, was typical of cultured, academic

thought in the days when the writer to the Hebrews wrote his letter.

Now, let us see the steps of the argument. It will be simpler if we list them one by one.

(1) The promise of the rest of God for his people still stands; the danger is that we fail to reach it.

(2) Long ago, the Israelites failed to enter into the rest of God. Here, the word *rest* is being used in the sense of the settlement of the promised land after the wilderness years. The reference is to Numbers 13 and 14. These chapters tell how the children of Israel came to the borders of the promised land, how they sent out scouts to spy out the land, how ten of the twelve scouts came back with the verdict that it was a good land but that the difficulties of entering into it were insuperable, how Caleb and Joshua alone were for going forward in the strength of the Lord, how the people listened to the advice of the cowards, and how the result was that that generation of distrusting cowards was barred forever from entering into the rest and the peace of the promised land. They did not trust God to bring them through the difficulties that lay ahead; and, therefore, they never enjoyed the rest they could have had.

(3) Now, the writer switches the meaning of the word *rest*. It is true that these people long ago missed the rest they might have had; but, although they missed it, *the rest remained.* Behind this argument lies one of the favourite conceptions of the Rabbis. On the seventh day, the day after creation had been completed, God rested from his labours. In the creation story in Genesis 1 and 2, there is a strange fact. On the first six days of creation, it is said that morning and evening came; that is to say, each day had an end and a beginning. But on the seventh day, the day of God's rest, *there is no mention of evening at all.* From this, the Rabbis argued that, while the

other days came to an end, the day of God's rest had no
ending; the rest of God was forever. Therefore, although long
ago the Israelites may have failed to enter that rest, it still
remained.

(4) Once again, the writer goes back to the meaning of
rest as the promised land. The day came after the forty years
of wandering in the wilderness when, under Joshua, the
people did enter into the promised land. Now, the promised
land was *the rest* and therefore it could be argued that then
the promise was fulfilled.

(5) But no, the promise is not fulfilled, because in Psalm
95:7–11 David hears God's voice saying to the people that if
they do not harden their hearts they can enter into his *rest*.
That is to say, hundreds of years *after* Joshua had led the
people into the *rest* of the promised land, God is *still* appealing
to them to enter into his *rest*. There is more to this *rest* than
merely entry into the promised land.

(6) So, the final appeal comes. God still appeals to people
not to harden their hearts but to enter into his rest. God's
'today' still exists and the promise is still open; but 'today'
does not last forever; life comes to an end; the promise can
be missed; therefore, says the writer to the Hebrews, 'Here
and now through faith enter into the very rest of God.'

There is a very interesting question of meaning in verse 1.
We have taken the translation: 'Beware lest any of you be
adjudged to have missed the rest of God.' That is to say:
'Beware that your disobedience and your lack of faith do not
mean that you have shut yourselves out from the rest and the
peace that God offers you.'

That may very well be the correct translation. But there is
another and most interesting possibility. The phrase may
mean: 'Beware of thinking that you have arrived too late in
history ever to enjoy the rest of God.'

44

In that second translation, there is a warning. It is very easy to think that the great days of religion are past. It is told that a child, on being told some of the great Old Testament stories, said wistfully: 'God was much more exciting then.' There is a continual tendency in the Church to look back, to believe that God's power has grown less and that the golden days have passed. The writer to the Hebrews sounds a trumpet-call. 'Never think', he says, 'that you have arrived too late in history; never think that the days of great promise and great achievement lie in the past. This is still God's "today". There is a blessedness for you as great as the blessedness of the saints; there is an adventure for you as great as the adventure of the martyrs. God is as great today as he ever was.'

There are two great permanent truths in this passage.

(1) A word, however great, has no impact unless it becomes integrated into the person who hears it. There are many different kinds of hearing in this world. There is indifferent hearing, uninterested hearing, critical hearing, sceptical hearing, cynical hearing. The hearing that matters is the hearing that listens eagerly, believes and acts. The promises of God are not merely beautiful pieces of literature; they are promises on which we are meant to stake our lives and which should dominate our actions.

(2) In the first verse, the writer to the Hebrews bids his people *beware* in case they miss the promise. The word we have translated as *beware* literally means *to fear* (*phobeisthai*). This Christian fear is not the fear which makes people run away from a task, nor the fear which reduces them to paralysed inaction; it is the fear which makes them summon every ounce of strength they possess in a great effort not to miss the one thing that is worth while.

THE TERROR OF THE WORD

Hebrews 4:11–13

> Let us then be eager to enter into that rest, lest we follow
> the example of the Israelites and fall into the same kind
> of disobedience. For the word of God is instinct with
> life; it is effective; it is sharper than a two-edged sword;
> it pierces right through to the very division of soul and
> spirit, joints and marrow; it scrutinizes the desires and
> intentions of the heart. No created thing can ever remain
> hidden from his sight; everything is naked to him and is
> compelled to meet the eyes of him with whom we have
> to reckon.

THE point of this passage is that the word of God has come,
and is such that it cannot be disregarded. The Jews always
had a very special idea about words. Once a word was spoken,
it had an independent existence. It was not only a sound with
a certain meaning; it was a power which went out and did
things. Isaiah heard God say that the word which went out of
his mouth would never be ineffective; it would always do
whatever he designed it to do (Isaiah 45:23).

We can understand something of this if we think of the
tremendous effect of words in history. A leader coins a
phrase and it becomes a trumpet-call which inspires people
to crusades or to crimes. Some great individual sends out a
manifesto and it produces action which can make or destroy
nations. Over and over again in history, the spoken word of
some leader or thinker has gone out and done things. If that
is so of human words, how much more is it so of the word of
God?

The writer to the Hebrews describes the word of God in a
series of great phrases. *The word of God is instinct with life*.
Certain issues are no longer of vital importance; certain books

and words have no living interest whatever. Plato was one of
the world's supreme thinkers, but it is unlikely that there
would be a huge public interest in Daily Studies in Plato. The
great fact about the word of God is that it is a living issue for
all people of all times. Other things may pass quietly into
oblivion; other things may acquire an academic or historical
interest; but the word of God is something that everyone must
face, and its offer is something we must accept or reject.

The word of God is *effective*. It is one of the facts of history
that, wherever people have taken God's word seriously, things
have begun to happen. When the English Bible was produced
and the word of God was made available to ordinary people,
the tremendous event of the Reformation inevitably followed.
When people take God seriously, they immediately realize
that his word is not only something to be studied, not only
something to be read, not only something to be written about;
it is something to be done.

The word of God is *penetrating*. The writer piles up phrases
to show how penetrating it is. It penetrates to the division of
soul and spirit. In Greek, the *psuchē*, the *soul*, is the essence
of life. All living things possess *psuchē*; it is physical life. In
Greek, the *pneuma*, the *spirit*, is that which is characteristic
of human beings. It is by spirit that we think and reason and
look beyond the earth to God. It is as if the writer to the
Hebrews were saying that the word of God tests our earthly
life and our spiritual existence. He says that the word of God
scrutinizes our *desires* and *intentions*. *Desire* (*enthumēsis*) is
the *emotional* part, and *intention* (*ennoia*) is the *intellectual*
part of every individual. It is as if he said: 'Your emotional
and intellectual life must both be submitted to the scrutiny of
God.'

Finally, the writer to the Hebrews sums things up. He says
that everything is *naked* to God and *compelled to meet his*

eyes. He uses two interesting words. The word for *naked* is the literal word (*gumnos*). What he is saying is that we may be able to wear our outward coverings and disguises; but in the presence of God these things are stripped away and we have to meet him as we are. The other word is even more vivid (*tetrachēlismenos*). This is not a common word, and its meaning is not quite certain. It seems to have been used in three different ways.

(1) It was a wrestler's word, and was used for seizing an opponent by the throat in such a way that he could not move. We may escape God for a while, but in the end he grips us in such a way that we cannot help meeting him face to face. God is one issue that no one can finally evade.

(2) It was the word that was used for flaying animals. Animals were hung up and the hide was taken off them. Other people may judge us by our outer conduct and appearance, but God sees into the innermost secrets of our hearts.

(3) Sometimes when a criminal was being led to judgment or to execution, a dagger, with point upwards, was fixed below his chin so that he could not bow his head to avoid being recognized, but had to keep it up so that all could see his face and know his dishonour. When that was done, the person was said to be *tetrachēlismenos*.

In the end, we have to meet the eyes of God. We may avert our gaze from people we are ashamed to meet; but we are *compelled* to look God in the face. The American sociologist Kermit Eby writes in *The God in You*: 'At some time or other, a man must stop running from himself and his God – possibly because there is just no other place to run to.' To each one of us, there comes a time when we have to meet that God from whose eyes nothing can ever be concealed.

THE PERFECT HIGH PRIEST

Hebrews 4:14–16

> Since then, we have a high priest, great in his nature,
> who has passed through the heavens, Jesus, the Son of
> God, let us hold fast to our creed. For we have not a
> high priest who is such that he cannot feel with us in
> our weaknesses; but one who has gone through every
> temptation, just in the same way as we have, and who
> is without sin. Let us then confidently approach his
> throne of grace, that we may receive mercy and find
> grace to help as need demands.

HERE, we are coming to closer grips with the great characteristic conception of Hebrews – that of Jesus as the perfect high priest. His task is to bring the voice of God to men and women, and to usher them into the presence of God. The high priest at one and the same time must perfectly know what it is to be human and also know God. That is what this epistle claims for Jesus.

(1) This passage begins by stressing the sheer greatness and absolute deity of Jesus. He is great in his nature, not by worldly honours or by any external trappings but in his own essential being. He has passed through the heavens. That may mean one of two things. In the New Testament, the word *heaven* is used in different ways. It can mean the heaven of the sky, and it can mean the heaven of the presence of God. This may mean that Jesus has passed through every heaven that may be and is in the very presence of God. It can mean what Christina Rossetti meant in the carol 'In the bleak midwinter' when she said: 'Heaven cannot hold Him.' Jesus is so great that even heaven is too small a place for him. No one ever stressed the sheer greatness of Jesus in the same way as the writer to the Hebrews.

(2) Then he turns to the other side. No one was ever surer of Jesus' complete identity with human beings. He went through everything that an individual has to go through and is like us in all things – except that he emerged from it all completely sinless. Before we turn to examine more closely the meaning of this, there is one thing we must note. The fact that Jesus was without sin means that he knew depths and tensions and assaults of temptation which we never can know. Far from his battle being easier, it was immeasurably harder. Why? For this reason – we fall to temptation long before the tempter has put out the whole of his power. We never know temptation at its fiercest because we fall long before that stage is reached. But Jesus was tempted far beyond anything we might experience; for in his case the tempter put everything he possessed into the attack. Think of this in terms of pain. There is a degree of pain which the human frame can stand – and, when that degree is passed, a person loses consciousness so that there are agonies of pain which are not realized. It is the same with temptation. Faced with temptation, we collapse; but Jesus went to our limit of temptation and far beyond it and still did not collapse. It is true to say that he was tempted in all things, just as we are; but it is also true to say that no one was tempted as he was.

(3) This experience of Jesus had three effects.

(a) It gave him *the gift of sympathy*. Here is something which we must understand but which we find very difficult. The Christian idea of God as a loving Father is interwoven into the very fabric of our mind and heart; but *it was a new idea*. To the Jews, the basic idea of God was that he was *holy* in the sense of being *different*. In no sense did he share our human experience – and he was in fact incapable of sharing it, simply because he was God.

It was even more so with the Greeks. The Stoics, the highest Greek thinkers, said that the primary attribute of God was *apatheia*, by which they meant essential inability to feel anything at all. They argued that if people could feel sorrow or joy, it meant that others were able to influence them. If so, the other people must, at least for that moment, be greater than they. No one, therefore, must be able in any sense to affect God, for that would be to make such a person greater than God; and so God had to be completely beyond all feeling. The other Greek school was the Epicureans. They held that the gods lived in perfect happiness and blessedness. They lived in what they called the *intermundia*, the spaces between the worlds; and they were not even aware of the world.

The Jews had their *different* God, the Stoics had their *feelingless* gods, and the Epicureans had their completely *detached* gods. Into that world of thought came Christianity with its incredible conception of a God who had deliberately undergone every human experience. Plutarch, one of the most religious of the Greeks, declared that it was blasphemous to involve God in the affairs of this world. Christianity depicted God as not so much involved but as identified with the suffering of this world. It is almost impossible for us to realize the revolution that Christianity brought about in the relationship of men and women to God. For century after century, they had been confronted with the idea of the untouchable God; and now they discovered a God who had gone through all that they must go through.

(b) That had two results. It gave God *the quality of mercy*. It is easy to see why. It was because God *understands*. Some people have lived sheltered lives; they have been protected from the temptations that come to those for whom life is not easy. Some people are placid and find it easy to control their emotions; others have a passionate nature that makes life more dangerous. The person who has lived the sheltered life and who has the more easy-going nature finds it hard to understand why the other person slips up. Such people are faintly disgusted and cannot help condemning what they cannot understand. *But God knows.* 'To know all is to forgive all' – of no one is that truer than of God.

Professor John Foster of Glasgow University told how he came into his home in this country one day in the 1930s to find his daughter, who was listening to the radio, in tears. He asked her why and found that the news bulletin had contained the sentence: 'Japanese tanks entered Canton today.' Most people would hear that with at the most a faint feeling of regret. Politicians may have heard it with grim foreboding; but to most people it did not make very much difference. Why was John Foster's daughter in tears? Because she had been born in Canton. To her, Canton meant a home, a nurse, a school, friends.

The difference was that *she had been there*. When you have been there, it makes all the difference. And there is no part of human experience of which God cannot say: 'I have been there.' When we have a sad and sorry tale to tell, when life has drenched us with tears, we do not go to a God who is incapable of understanding what has happened; we go to a God who has been there. That is why – if we may put it in this way – God finds it easy to forgive.

(c) It makes God *able to help*. He knows our problems because he has come through them. The best person to give you advice and help on a journey is someone who has already travelled that way. God can help because he knows it all.

Jesus is the perfect high priest because he is perfectly God, and perfectly one with us. Because he has known our life, he can give us sympathy, mercy and power. He brought God to men and women, and he can bring them to God.

AT HOME WITH THE WORLD
AND WITH GOD

Hebrews 5:1–10

Every high priest who is chosen from among men is appointed on men's behalf to deal with the things which concern God. His task is to offer gifts and sacrifices for sins, in that he himself is able to feel gently to the ignorant and to the wandering because he himself wears the garment of human weakness. By reason of this very weakness it is incumbent upon him, just as he makes sacrifice for the people, so to make sacrifice for sins on his own behalf also. No one takes this honourable position to himself, but he is called by God to it, just as Aaron was. So it was not Christ who gave himself the glory of becoming high priest; but it was God who said to him: 'You are my beloved Son; today I have begotten you.' Just so, he says also in another passage: 'You are a priest forever according to the order of Melchizedek.' In the days when he lived this human life of ours, he offered prayers and entreaties to him who was able to bring him safely through death with strong crying and with tears. And when he had been heard because of his reverence, although he was a Son, he learned obedience from the sufferings through which he passed. When he had been made fully fit for his appointed task, he became the author of eternal salvation to all who obey him, for he had been designated by God a high priest after the order of Melchizedek.

Now, Hebrews comes to work out the doctrine which is its special contribution to Christian thought – the doctrine of the high priesthood of Jesus Christ. This passage sets out three essential qualifications of the priest in any age and in any generation.

(1) Priests are appointed on behalf of others to deal with the things concerning God. Professor A. J. Gossip of Trinity College, Glasgow, used to tell his students that when he was ordained to the ministry he felt as if the people were saying to him: 'We are forever involved in the dust and the heat of the day; we have to spend our time getting and spending; we have to serve at the counter, to toil at the desk, to make the wheels of industry go round. We want you to be set apart so that you can go in to the secret place of God and come back every Sunday with a word from him to us.' The priest is the link between God and the world.

In Israel, the priest had one special function – to offer sacrifice for the sins of the people. Sin disturbs the relationship which should exist between men and women and God and puts up a barrier between them. The sacrifice is meant to restore that relationship and remove that barrier.

But we must note that the Jews were always quite clear that the sins for which sacrifice could atone were *sins of ignorance*. The deliberate sin did not find its atonement in sacrifice. The writer to the Hebrews himself says: 'For if we wilfully persist in sin after having received the knowledge of the truth, *there no longer remains a sacrifice for sins*' (Hebrews 10:26). This is a conviction that emerges again and again in the sacrificial laws of the Old Testament. Again and again, they begin: 'When anyone sins unintentionally in any of the Lord's commandments about things not to be done . . .' (Leviticus 4:2, cf. verse 13). Numbers 15:22–31 is a key passage. There, the necessary sacrifices are laid down 'if you unintentionally fail to observe all these commandments'. But at the end it is laid down: 'But whoever acts high-handedly . . . affronts the Lord . . . shall be utterly cut off and bear the guilt.' Deuteronomy 17:12 lays it down: 'Anyone who presumes to disobey . . . that person shall die.'

The sin of ignorance is pardonable; the sin of presumption is not. Nevertheless, we must note that by the sin of ignorance the Jews meant more than simply lack of knowledge. They included the sins committed when someone was carried away in a moment of impulse or anger or passion or was overcome by some irresistible temptation, and the sins were followed by repentance. By the sin of presumption, they meant the cold, calculated sin for which the perpetrator was not in the least sorry, the open-eyed disobedience of God.

So, the priest existed to open for sinners the way back to God – as long as they wanted to come back.

(2) Priests must be at one with others. They must have gone through the same experiences and must be in full sympathy with others. At this point, the writer to the Hebrews stops to point out – he will later show that this is one of the ways in which Jesus Christ is superior to any earthly priest – that earthly priests are so at one with other people that they have an obligation to offer sacrifice for their own sin before they offer sacrifice for the sins of others. Priests must be bound up with other men and women in all that life brings. In connection with this, the writer used a wonderful word – *metriopathein*. We have translated it as *to feel gently*; but it is really untranslatable.

The Greeks defined a virtue as the mid-point between two extremes. On either hand, there was an extreme into which people might fall; in between, there was the right way. So, the Greeks defined *metriopatheia* (the corresponding noun) as the mid-point between extravagant grief and utter indifference. It was feeling about others in the right way. W. M. Macgregor, Principal of Trinity College, Glasgow, defined it as 'the mid-course between explosions of anger and lazy indulgence'. The Greek philosopher and historian Plutarch spoke of that *patience* which was the child of *metriopatheia*.

He spoke of it as that sympathetic feeling which enabled people to lift up and to save, to spare and to hear. Another Greek blames a man for having no *metriopatheia* and for therefore *refusing to be reconciled* with someone who had differed from him. It is a wonderful word. It means the ability to put up with people without getting irritated; it means the ability not to lose one's temper with people when they are foolish and will not learn and do the same thing over and over again. It describes the attitude which does not get angry at the faults of others and which does not condone them, but which to the end of the day devotes itself to offering gentle yet powerful sympathy which by its very patience directs people back to the right way. We can never deal with others unless we have this strong and patient, God-given *metriopatheia*.

(3) The third essential characteristic of a priest is this: people do not appoint themselves to the priesthood; their appointment is from God. The priesthood is not an office which is taken; it is a privilege and a glory to which people are called. The ministry of God is neither a job nor a career but a calling. Those who are called to the priesthood ought to be able to look back and say not: 'I chose this work' but rather: 'God chose me and gave me this work to do.'

The writer to the Hebrews goes on to show how Jesus Christ fulfils the great conditions of the priesthood.

(1) He takes the last one first. Jesus did not choose his task; God chose him for it. At his baptism, there came to Jesus the voice which said: 'You are my son; today I have begotten you' (Psalm 2:7).

(2) Jesus has gone through the most bitter human experiences and understands what it is to be human with all its strength and weakness. The writer to the Hebrews has four great thoughts about him.

(a) He remembers Jesus in Gethsemane. That is what he is thinking of when he speaks of Jesus' prayers and entreaties, his tears and his cry. The word he uses for *cry* (*kraugē*) is very significant. It is an involuntary sound, a cry that is uttered in the stress of some tremendous tension or searing pain. So, the writer to the Hebrews says that there is no agony of the human spirit through which Jesus has not come. The Rabbis had a saying: 'There are three kinds of prayers, each loftier than the preceding – prayer, crying and tears. Prayer is made in silence; crying with raised voice; but tears overcome all things.' Jesus knew even the desperate prayer of tears.

(b) Jesus learned from all his experiences because he met them all with reverence. The Greek phrase for 'He learned from what he suffered' is a linguistic jingle – *emathen aph' hōn epathen*. And this is an idea which keeps recurring in the Greek thinkers. They are always connecting *mathein*, to learn, and *pathein*, to suffer. Aeschylus, the earliest of the great Greek dramatists, had as a kind of continual text: 'Learning comes from suffering' (*pathei mathos*). He calls suffering a kind of *savage grace* from the gods. Herodotus declared that his sufferings were *acharista mathēmata*, ungracious ways of learning. A traditional Irish proverb says of the poets:

We learn in suffering what we teach in song.

God speaks to us in many experiences of life, and not least in those which try our hearts and souls. But we can hear his voice only when we accept in reverence what comes to us. If we accept it with resentment, the rebellious cries of our own hearts make us deaf to the voice of God.

(c) By means of the experiences through which he passed, both the Authorized and the Revised Standard Versions say that Jesus *was made perfect* (*teleioun*). *Teleioun* is the verb of the adjective *teleios*. *Teleios* can quite correctly be

57

translated as *perfect* as long as we remember what the Greeks understood by that perfection. In Greek thought, a thing was *teleios* if it perfectly carried out the purpose for which it was designed. When people used the word, they were not thinking in terms of abstract and metaphysical perfection; they were thinking in terms of *function*. What the writer to the Hebrews is saying is that all the experiences of suffering through which Jesus passed perfectly fitted him to become the Saviour of the world.

(d) The salvation which Jesus brought is an *eternal salvation*. It is something which keeps people safe both in the present time and in eternity. With Christ, we are safe forever. There are no circumstances that can snatch us from Christ's hand.

THE REFUSAL TO GROW UP

Hebrews 5:11–14

> The story which has been laid upon me to tell you about this matter is a long story, difficult to tell and difficult to grasp, for your ears have become dull. For, indeed, at a stage when you ought to be teachers because of the length of time that has passed since you first heard the gospel, you still need someone to tell you the simple elements of the very beginning of the message of God. You have sunk into a state when you need milk and not solid food; for when anyone is at the stage of participating in milk feeding, he does not really know what Christian righteousness is, for he is only a child. For solid food is for those who have reached maturity, those who, through the development of the right kind of habit, have reached a stage when their perceptions are trained to distinguish between good and evil.

HERE, the writer to the Hebrews deals with the difficulties which confront him in attempting to get across an adequate conception of Christianity to his hearers.

He is confronted with two difficulties. First, the Christian faith in all its fullness is by no means an easy thing to grasp, nor can it be learned in a day. Second, the hearing of his hearers is *dull*. The word he uses (*nōthros*) is full of meaning. It means slow-moving in mind, sluggish in understanding, dull of hearing, stupidly forgetful. It can be used of the numbed limbs of an animal which is ill. It can be used of a person who has the imperceptive nature of a stone. Now, this has something to say to everyone whose business it is to preach and to teach; in fact, it has something to say to everyone whose business it is to think, and that means that it has something to say to everyone. It often happens that we avoid teaching some elements because they are difficult; we defend ourselves by saying that our hearers would never grasp such ideas. It is one of the tragedies of the Church that there is so little attempt to teach new knowledge and new thinking. It is true that such teaching is difficult. It is true that it often means meeting the lethargy of the lazy mind and the defensive prejudice of the shut mind. But the task remains. The writer to the Hebrews did not seek to avoid the duty of bringing his message, even if it was difficult and the minds of his hearers were slow. He regarded it as his supreme responsibility to pass on the truth he knew.

His complaint is that his hearers have been Christians for many years and are still babes no nearer maturity. The contrast between the immature Christian and the child, between milk and solid food, often occurs in the New Testament (1 Peter 2:2; 1 Corinthians 2:6, 3:2, 14:20; Ephesians 4:13ff.). Hebrews says that by now they should be teachers. It is not necessary to take that literally. To say that someone was able to teach was the Greek way of saying that that person had a mature grasp of a subject. The writer says that they still need someone to teach them *the simple elements (stoicheia) of Christianity*. This word has a variety of meanings. In grammar, it means the letters of the alphabet, the A B C; in physics, it means the four basic elements of which the world is composed; in geometry, it means the elements of proof, like the point and the straight line; in philosophy, it means the first elementary principles with which the students begin. It is the sorrow of the writer to the Hebrews that, after many years of Christianity, his people have never got past the basics; they are like children who do not know the difference between right and wrong.

Here, he is face to face with a problem which confronts the Church in every generation – that of *Christians who refuse to grow up*.

(1) Christians can refuse to grow up in knowledge. They can be guilty of failure to take the opportunities that broaden horizons and develop ideas. There are people who keep on saying that what was good enough for people in the past is good enough for them. There are Christians in whose faith there has been no development for thirty or forty or fifty or sixty years. There are Christians who have deliberately refused to try to understand the advances that biblical scholarship and theological thought have made. They are grown men and women, and yet they insist on remaining content with the religious development of children.

They are like surgeons who refuse to use the new techniques of surgery, refuse to use the new anaesthetics, refuse to use any new equipment and say: 'What was good enough for Lister in the nineteenth century is good enough for me.' They are like a physician who refuses to use any of the new drugs and says: 'What I learned as a student fifty years ago is good enough for me.' In religious matters, it is even worse. God is infinite; the riches of Christ are unsearchable; and to the end of the day we should be moving forward.

(2) There are people who have never grown up in behaviour. It may be forgivable in a child to sulk or to throw fits of temper, but there are many adults who are just as childish in their behaviour.

A case of arrested development is always pathetic to see; and the world is full of people whose religious development has been arrested. They stopped learning years ago, and their conduct is that of a child. It is true that Jesus said the greatest thing in the world is the *childlike* spirit; but there is a tremendous difference between the *childlike* and the *childish* spirit. Peter Pan makes a charming play on the stage, but the person who will not grow up makes a tragedy in real life. Let us take care that we do not remain in the religion of childhood when we should have reached the faith of maturity.

THE NECESSITY OF PROGRESS

Hebrews 6:1–3

> So, then, let us leave elementary teaching about Christ behind us and let us be borne onwards to full maturity; for we cannot go on laying the foundations all the time and teaching about repentance from dead works and giving information about washings, about the laying on of hands, about the resurrection from the dead and upon that sentence which lasts to all eternity. God willing, this very thing we will do.

THE writer to the Hebrews was certain of the necessity of progress in the Christian life. Teachers would never get anywhere if they had to lay the foundations all over again every time they began to teach. The writer to the Hebrews says that his people must be going on to what he calls *teleiotēs*. The Authorized Version translates this word as *perfection*. But *teleios*, the adjective, and its kindred words have a technical meaning. Pythagoras divided his students into *hoi manthanontes*, *the learners*, and *hoi teleioi*, *the mature*. Philo divided his students into three different classes – *hoi archomenoi*, *those just beginning*, *hoi prokoptontes*, *those making progress*, and *hoi teleiōmenoi*, *those beginning to reach maturity*. *Teleiotēs* does not imply complete knowledge but a certain maturity in the Christian faith.

The writer to the Hebrews means two things by this *maturity*.

(1) He means something to do with *the mind*. He means that as people get older they should more and more have thought things out for themselves. They should, for instance, be able to say better who they believe Jesus to be. They should have a deeper grasp not only of the facts but also of the significances of the Christian faith.

(2) He means something to do with *life*. As people grow older, their lives should more and more reflect Christ. All the time, they should be ridding themselves of old faults and achieving new virtues. Daily, a new serenity and a new nobility should be breaking upon life. As Karle Wilson has it in her poem 'Old Lace':

> Let me grow lovely, growing old;
>   So many fine things do,
> Laces and Ivory and Gold and Silks,
>   Need not be new.
> And there is healing in old trees,
>   Old streets and glamour old,
> Why may not I, as well as these,
>   Grow lovely, growing old?

There can be no standing still in the Christian life. It is told that, on his pocket Bible, the Lord Protector of England, Oliver Cromwell, had a motto written in Latin – *qui cessat esse melior cessat esse bonus* – he who ceases to be better ceases to be good.

This passage enables us to see what the early Church regarded as basic Christianity.

(1) There is *repentance from dead works*. The Christian life begins with *repentance*, and repentance (*metanoia*) is literally *a change of mind*. There is a new attitude to God, to other people, to life, to self. It is a repentance from *dead works*. What does the writer to the Hebrews mean by this strange phrase? There are many things that he may mean, and each of them is relevant and thought-provoking. (a) Dead works may be *deeds which bring death*. They may be the immoral, selfish, godless, loveless, soiled actions which lead to death. (b) They may be *defiling deeds*. For a Jew, to touch a dead body was the greatest defilement; to do so rendered him unclean and barred him from the worship of God until he was cleansed. Dead works may be those which bring defilement and separate people from God. (c) They may be *works which have no connection with character*. For the Jews, life was ritual; if they observed the proper ceremonies at the right time, they were considered good. But none of these things had any effect upon an individual's character. It may be that the writer to the Hebrews means that Christians have broken away from the meaningless rituals and conventions of life to give themselves to the things which deepen character and develop the soul.

(2) There is *faith which looks to God*. The first essential in the Christian life is the godward look. Christians determine their actions not by the verdict of others but by the verdict of God. They look not to their own achievements for salvation but to the grace of God.

(3) There is *teaching about washings*. This means that Christians must realize what baptism really means. The first book of Christian instruction for those about to enter the Church and the first service order book is a little book called the *Didache*: *The Teaching* of *the Twelve Apostles*. It was written about the year AD 100 and lays down the regulations for Christian baptism. Now, at this time, infant baptism had not yet emerged. People were coming straight from paganism, and baptism was reception into the Church and confession of faith. The *Didache* begins with six short chapters on the Christian faith and the Christian life. It begins by telling candidates for baptism what they ought to believe and how they ought to live. Then, in the seventh chapter, it goes on:

> Concerning Baptism, baptize in this way. When you have instructed the candidate in all these things, baptize in the name of the Father and of the Son and of the Holy Spirit in running water. If you do not have running water, baptize in any other kind of water. If you cannot baptize in cold water, baptize in warm. If both of these are unobtainable, pour water three times upon the head of the candidate in the name of the Father and of the Son and of the Holy Spirit. Before baptism, let him who is to baptize and him who is to be baptized fast, and let any others who can do so do the same. You must bid him who is to be baptized to fast for two or three days before the ceremony.

That is interesting. It shows that baptism in the early Church was, if possible, by total immersion. It shows that those to be baptized were either immersed or had the water poured over them three times, in the name of the Father, of the Son and of the Holy Spirit. It shows that baptism was instructed baptism, for the account of the Christian faith and life is to be repeated before the sacrament of baptism is carried out. It shows that candidates for baptism had to prepare not only their minds but also their spirit, for they had to fast beforehand. In the early days, no one slipped into the Church without knowing what they were doing. So, the writer to the Hebrews says: 'At your baptism, you were instructed in the basis of the Christian faith. There is no need to go back to that. You must build a fuller faith on the basis you have already laid down.'

(4) There is *the laying on of hands*. In Jewish practice, the laying on of hands was significant in three ways. (a) It was the sign of the transference of guilt. Those making the sacrifice laid their hands upon the head of the victim to symbolize the fact that they transferred their guilt to the animals being offered. (b) It was the sign of the transference of blessing. When a father blessed his son, he laid his hands on the son's head as a token of that blessing. (c) It was the sign of setting apart to some special office. Individuals were ordained to office by the laying on of hands.

In the early Church, it always accompanied baptism and was the way in which the Holy Spirit was conveyed to the person newly baptized (Acts 8:17, 19:6). This is not to be thought of in a material way. In those days, the apostles were regarded with reverence because they had actually been the friends of Jesus on earth. It was a thrilling thing to be touched by someone who had actually touched the hand of Jesus. The effect of the laying on of hands depends not on the office of the one who lays on the hands but on that person's character and nearness to Christ.

(5) There is *the resurrection from the dead*. From the beginning, Christianity was a religion of immortality. It gave people two worlds in which to live; it taught them that the best was yet to be and thereby made this world the training school for eternity.

(6) There is *the sentence which lasts to all eternity*. Christianity was from the beginning a religion of judgment. Christians were never allowed to forget that in the end they must face God, and that what God thought of them was infinitely more important than what other people thought of them.

CRUCIFYING CHRIST AGAIN

Hebrews 6:4–8

> For it is impossible to renew to repentance those who were once enlightened, those who tasted the free gift from heaven, those who were made sharers in the Holy Spirit, those who tasted the fair word of God and the powers of the age to come, and who then became apostates, for they are crucifying the Son of God again for themselves and are making a mocking show of him. For when the earth has drunk the rain that comes often upon it and when it brings forth herbage useful to those who cultivate it, it receives a share of blessing from God; but if it produces thorns and thistles it is rejected and is in imminent danger of a curse, and its end is to be appointed for burning.

THIS is one of the most terrible passages in Scripture. It begins with a kind of list of the privileges of the Christian life.

Christians have been *enlightened*. This is a favourite New Testament idea. No doubt it goes back to the picture of Jesus as the light of the world, the light that enlightens everyone (John 1:9, 9:5). As Thomas Bilney, the sixteenth-century Protestant martyr, said: 'When I heard the words, "Christ Jesus came into the world to save sinners," it was as if day suddenly broke in the midst of a dark night.' The light of knowledge and joy and guidance breaks in upon men and women with Christ. So entwined with this idea did Christianity become that *enlightenment (phōtismos)* became a synonym for *baptism*, and *to be enlightened (phōtizesthai)* became a synonym for *to be baptized*. That is, in fact, the way many people have read this word here; and they have taken this passage to mean that there is no possibility of forgiveness for sins committed after baptism; and there have been times and places in the Church when baptism has been postponed to the moment of death in order to be safe. We shall discuss that idea later.

Christians have tasted *the free gift that comes from heaven.* It is only in Christ that we can be at peace with God. Forgiveness is not something we can ever win; it is a free gift. It is only when we come to the cross that our burden is rolled away. Christians are men and women who know the immeasurable relief of experiencing the free gift of the forgiveness of God.

Christians are *sharers in the Holy Spirit.* They have a new directive and a new power in their lives. They have discovered the presence of a power that can both tell them what to do and enable them to do it.

Christians have *tasted the fair word of God.* That is another way of saying that they have discovered the truth. It is a human characteristic instinctively to follow truth as the blind long for light; it is part of the penalty and the privilege of being human that we can never rest content until we have learned the meaning of life. In God's word, we find the truth and the meaning of life.

Christians have *tasted the powers of the world to come.* Both Jews and Christians divided time into two ages. There was this present age (*ho nun aiōn*), which was wholly bad; and there was the age to come (*ho mellōn aiōn*), which would be wholly good. Some day, God would intervene; there would come the shattering destruction and the terrible judgment of the day of the Lord, and then this present age would end and the age to come would begin. But Christians are men and women who here and now are tasting the blessedness of the age which is God's. Even in the present time, they have a foretaste of eternity. As George Wade Robertson's hymn has it:

> Heaven above is softer blue,
>   Earth around is sweeter green;
> Something lives in every hue,
>   Christless eyes have never seen;
> Birds with gladder songs o'erflow,
>   Flowers with deeper beauties shine,
> Since I know, as now I know,
>   I am his, and he is mine.

So, the writer to the Hebrews sets out the shining catalogue of Christian blessedness; and then at the end of it there comes, like a sudden knell, *who then became apostates* – who rejected the faith.

What does he mean when he says that it is impossible that those who have become apostates can ever be renewed to repentance? Many commentators have tried to find a way round this word *impossible* (*adunaton*). The Dutch reformer Erasmus held that it was to be taken in the sense of difficult almost to the point of impossibility. The eighteenth-century German scholar Johannes Bengel held that what was impossible for us was possible for God, and that we must leave those who have fallen away to the mercy of God's exceptional love. But, when we read this passage, we must remember that *it was written in an age of persecution*, and in any such age apostasy is the supreme sin. In any age of persecution, people can save their lives by denying Christ; but every person who does so aims a body-blow at the Church, for it means that such people have counted their lives and comfort dearer to them than Jesus Christ.

This particular way of putting things has always emerged during and after persecutions. Some 200 years after this came the terrible persecution by the Emperor Diocletian. When peace came after the storm, the one test some wanted to apply to every surviving member of the Church was: 'Did you deny Christ and so save your life?' And, if any had denied their Lord, they would have shut the door on them once and for all. The sociologist Kermit Eby tells of a French churchman who, when asked what he did during the French Revolution, whispered: 'I survived.'

This is the condemnation of those who loved life more than they loved Christ. It was never meant to be built up into a doctrine that there is no forgiveness for post-baptismal sin. Who can possibly say that another person is beyond the forgiveness of God? What it is meant to show is the terrible seriousness of choosing existence instead of loyalty to Christ.

The writer to the Hebrews goes on to say a tremendous thing. Those who fall away *crucify Christ again*. This is the point of the great *Quo vadis* legend. It tells how, in the Neronic persecution, Peter was caught in Rome and his courage failed. Down the Appian Way, he fled for his life. Suddenly, there was a figure standing in his path. It was Jesus himself. '*Domine*,' said Peter, '*quo vadis?* Lord, where are you going?' 'I am going back to Rome to be crucified again, this time in your place.' And Peter, shamed into heroism, turned back to Rome and died a martyr's death.

Late in Roman history, there was an emperor who tried to put back the clock. Julian wanted to destroy Christianity and bring back the old gods. His attempt ended in defeat. The playwright Henrik Ibsen makes him say: 'Where is he now?

Has he been at work elsewhere since *that* happened at Golgotha? . . . Where is he now? What if *that*, at Golgotha, near Jerusalem, was but a wayside matter, a thing done, as it were, in the passing? What if he goes on and on, suffers and dies and conquers again and again, from world to world?'

There is a certain truth there. Behind the thought of the writer to the Hebrews, there is a tremendous conception. He saw the cross as an event which opened a window into the heart of God. He saw it as showing in a moment of time the suffering love which is forever in that heart. The cross said to men and women: 'That is how I have always loved you and always will love you. This is what your sin does to me and always will do to me. This is the only way I can ever redeem you.'

As long as there is sin, there is always in God's heart this agony of suffering and redeeming love. Sin does not only break God's law; it breaks his heart. It is true that, when we fall away, we crucify Christ again.

Further, the writer to the Hebrews says that, when we fall away, we make *a mocking show of Christ*. How is that? When we sin, the world will say: 'So that is all that Christianity is worth. So that is all this Christ can do. So that is all the cross achieved.' It is bad enough that, when a church member falls into sin, he or she brings personal shame and discredit on the Church; but what is worse is that the sin of one individual brings taunts and jeers of others upon *Christ*.

We may note a final thing. It has been pointed out that in the letter to the Hebrews there are four impossible things. There is the impossibility of this passage. The other three are: (1) It is impossible for God to lie (6:18). (2) It is impossible that the blood of bulls and goats should take away sin (10:4). (3) Without faith, it is impossible to please God (11:6).

THE BRIGHTER SIDE

Hebrews 6:9–12

> Beloved, even if we do speak like this, we are persuaded
> of better things for you, yes, things that are bound up
> with salvation. For God is not unjust to forget your work
> and the love that you displayed in that you have been
> and still are active in the service of God's dedicated
> people. We hope with all our hearts that each one of
> you will display the same zeal to make your hope
> come true and that you will go on doing so until the
> end, so that you may not become lazily lethargic but
> may copy those who through faith and patience inherit
> the promises.

ONE thing stands out here. This is the only passage in the
whole letter where the writer addresses his people as *beloved*.
It is precisely after the sternest passage of all that he uses the
address of love. It is as if he said to them: 'If I did not love
you so much, I would not speak with such severity.' The
fourth-century scholar John Chrysostom paraphrases the
thought this way: 'It is better that I should scare you with
words than that you should sorrow in deeds.' The writer
speaks the truth; but, however stern it may be, he speaks it in
love.

Further, his very form of speaking shows how individual
his love is. 'We hope', he says, 'that *each one of you* will
display the zeal that will make your hope come true.' He is
thinking of them not as a crowd but as individual men and
women. Dr Paul Tournier in *A Doctor's Casebook* has a
paragraph on what he calls *the personalism* of the Bible. 'God
says to Moses, "I know you by name" (Exodus 33:17). He
says to Cyrus, "It is I, the Lord, who call you by your name"
(Isaiah 45:3). One is struck, on reading the Bible, by the

importance in it of personal names. Whole chapters are devoted to long genealogies. When I was young I used to think that they could well have been dropped from the Biblical Canon. But I have since realized that these series of proper names bear witness to the fact that, in the biblical perspective, man is neither a thing nor an abstraction, not a fraction of the mass, as the Marxists see him, but a person.' When the writer to the Hebrews wrote with sternness, he was not rebuking a church; he was yearning over individual men and women, as God himself does.

There are two interesting things implicit in this passage.

(1) We learn that, even if these people to whom he is writing have failed to grow up in Christian faith and knowledge, and even if they have been falling away from their first enthusiasm, they have never given up their practical service to their fellow Christians. There is a great practical truth here. Sometimes, in the Christian life, we come to times which are arid; the church services have nothing to say to us, the teaching that we do in Sunday School or the singing that we do in the choir or the service we give on a committee becomes a labour without joy. At such a time, there are two alternatives. We can give up our worship and our service; but, if we do, we are lost. Or we can go determinedly on with them, and the strange thing is that the light and the attractiveness and the joy will in time come back again. In the arid times, the best thing to do is to go on with the habits of the Christian life and of the Church. If we do, we can be sure that the sun will shine again.

(2) He tells his people to be imitators of those who through faith and patience inherited the promise. What he is saying to them is: 'You are not the first to launch out on the glories and the perils of the Christian faith. Others braved the dangers and endured the tribulations before you and won through.'

He is telling them to go on in the realization that others have gone through their struggle and won the victory. Christians are not treading an untrodden pathway; they are treading where the saints have trod.

THE SURE HOPE

Hebrews 6:13–20

> When God made his promise to Abraham, since he was not able to swear by anyone greater, he swore by himself. 'Certainly,' he said, 'I will bless you and I will multiply you.' When Abraham had thus exercised patience, he received the promise. Men swear by someone who is greater than themselves; and an oath serves for a guarantee beyond all possibility of contradiction. But on this occasion God, in his quite exceptional desire to make clear to the heirs of the promise the unalterable character of his intention, interposed with an oath, so that by two unalterable things, in which it is impossible that God should lie, we, who have fled to him for refuge, might be strongly encouraged to lay hold upon the hope that is set before us. This hope is to us like an anchor, safe and sure, and it enters with us into the inner court beyond the veil, where Jesus has already entered as a forerunner for us, when he became a high priest forever after the order of Melchizedek.

GOD made more than one promise to Abraham. Genesis 12:7 tells us of the one made when he called him out of Ur and sent him into the unknown and to the promised land. Genesis 17:5–6 is the promise of many descendants who would be blessed in him. Genesis 18:18 is a repetition of that promise. But the promise which God swore with an oath to keep comes in Genesis 22:16–18. The real meaning of this first sentence is: 'God made many promises to Abraham, and in the end he actually made one which he confirmed with an oath.' That promise was, as it were, doubly binding. It was God's word which in itself made it sure, but in addition it was confirmed by an oath. Now, that promise was that all Abraham's descendants would be blessed; therefore, that promise was to the Christian Church, for the Church was the true Israel and the true seed of Abraham. That blessing came true in Jesus Christ. Abraham certainly had to exercise patience before he received the promise. It was not until twenty-five years after he had left Ur that his son Isaac was born. He was old; Sarah was barren; the wandering was long; but Abraham never wavered from his hope and trust in the promise of God.

In the ancient world, the *anchor* was the symbol of hope. The Stoic philosopher Epictetus says: 'A ship should never depend on one anchor, or a life on one hope.' Pythagoras the mathematician said: 'Wealth is a weak anchor; fame is still weaker. What then are the anchors which are strong? Wisdom, great-heartedness, courage – these are the anchors which no storm can shake.' The writer to the Hebrews insists that Christians possess the greatest hope in the world.

That hope, he says, is one which enters into the inner court beyond the veil. In the Temple, the most sacred of all places was the Holy of Holies. The veil was what covered it. It was believed that anyone who entered the Holy of Holies entered into the very presence of God, and into that place only one man in all the world could go. That man was the high priest; and even he might enter that holy place on only one day of the year, the Day of Atonement.

Even then, it was laid down, he must not linger in it, for it was a dangerous and a terrible thing to enter into the presence of the living God. What the writer to the Hebrews says is this: 'Under the old Jewish religion, no one might enter into the presence of God but the high priest and he only on one day of the year; but now Jesus Christ has opened the way for every individual at every time.'

The writer to the Hebrews uses a most illuminating word about Jesus. He says that he entered the presence of God as our *forerunner*. The word is *prodromos*. It has three stages of meaning. (1) It means *one who rushes on*. (2) It means *a pioneer*. (3) It means a scout who goes ahead to see that it is safe for the rest of the troops to follow. Jesus went into the presence of God to make it safe for all to follow.

Let us put it very simply in another way. Before Jesus came, God was the distant stranger whom only a very few might approach, and that at peril of their lives. But, because of what Jesus was and did, God has become the friend of all. Once, people thought of him as barring the door; now, they think of the door to his presence as thrown wide open to all.

A PRIEST AFTER THE
ORDER OF MELCHIZEDEK

Hebrews 7

WE come now to a passage of such supreme importance for the writer to the Hebrews and in itself so difficult to understand that we must deal with it in a special way. Chapter 6 ended with the statement that Jesus had been made a priest forever after the order of Melchizedek. This priesthood after the order of Melchizedek is the most characteristic thought of Hebrews. Behind it lie ways of thinking and of arguing and of using Scripture which are quite strange to us and which we must try to understand. It will be best first to collect together all that the writer to the Hebrews has to say about the priesthood after the order of Melchizedek and to read that

as a whole before we divide it into shorter passages to study
in detail. We shall then try to understand what the writer to
the Hebrews was getting at before we study this chapter in
detail.

So, we collect the passages which deal with this idea. The
first is Hebrews 5:1–10.

> Every high priest who is chosen from among men is
> appointed on men's behalf to deal with the things which
> concern God. His task is to offer gifts and sacrifices for
> sins, in that he himself is able to feel gently to the
> ignorant and to the wandering because he himself wears
> the garment of human weakness. By reason of this very
> weakness it is incumbent upon him, just as he makes
> sacrifice for the people, so to make sacrifice for sins on
> his own behalf also. No one takes this honourable
> position to himself, but he is called by God to it, just as
> Aaron was. So it was not Christ who gave himself the
> glory of becoming high priest; but it was God who said
> to him: 'You are my beloved Son; today I have begotten
> you.' Just so, he says also in another passage: 'You are
> a priest forever according to the order of Melchizedek.'
> In the days when he lived this human life of ours, he
> offered prayers and entreaties to him who was able to
> bring him safely through death with strong crying and
> with tears. And when he had been heard because of his
> reverence, although he was a Son, he learned obedience
> from the sufferings through which he passed. When he
> had been made fully fit for his appointed task, he became
> the author of eternal salvation to all who obey him, for
> he had been designated by God *a high priest after the
> order of Melchizedek.*

The second passage which deals with this idea is the whole
of Hebrews 7. So, first, let us set it down as a whole,
remembering that the last verse of Hebrews 6 has already

said that Jesus had become *a high priest forever after the order* of *Melchizedek.*

Now this Melchizedek was King of Salem and priest of the most high God. He met Abraham when he was returning from the smiting of the kings and blessed him, and Abraham set apart for him a tenth part of the spoils. In the first place, the interpretation of his own name means King of Righteousness and, in the second place, King of Salem means King of Peace. His father is never mentioned nor his mother; nor is there any record of his descent; there is no mention of the beginning of his days nor any of the end of his life; he is exactly like the Son of God; and he remains a priest forever.

Just see how great this man was – Abraham gave him the tenth part of the spoils of victory – and Abraham was no less than the founder of our nation. Now look at the difference – when the sons of Levi receive their priesthood, they receive an injunction laid down by the law to exact tithes from the people. That is to say, they exact tithes from their own brothers, even although they are descendants of Abraham. But this man, whose descent is not traced through them at all, exacted tithes from Abraham and actually blessed the man who had received the promises. Beyond all argument, the lesser is blessed by the greater. Just so, in the one instance, it is a case of men who die receiving tithes; but, in this instance, it is the case of a man whom the evidence proves to live. Still further – if I may put it this way – through Abraham, Levi, too, the very man who receives the tithes, had tithes exacted from him, for he was in his father's body when Melchizedek met him.

If, then, the desired effect could have been achieved by the Levitical priesthood – for it was on the basis of it that the people became a people of the law – what further need was there to set up another priest and to call him a priest after the order of Melchizedek, and not to call him a priest after the order of Aaron? Once the priesthood was altered, of necessity there follows an alteration of the law too, for the person of whom the statements are made belongs to another tribe altogether, from which no one ever served at the altar. It is obvious that it was from Judah that our Lord sprang, and, with regard to that tribe, Moses said nothing about priests. And certain things are still more abundantly clear – if a different priest is set up, a priest after the order of Melchizedek, a priest who has become so, not according to the law of a mere human injunction but according to the power of a life that is indestructible – for the witness of Scripture in regard to this is: 'You are a priest forever after the order of Melchizedek' – if all that is so, two things emerge. On the one hand, there emerges the cancellation of the previous injunction because of its own weakness and uselessness (for the law never achieved the effect which it was designed to produce) and, on the other hand, there emerges the introduction of a better hope through which we can come near to God.

And inasmuch as it happened with an oath – for the Levitical priests are made priests without an oath, but he with an oath, because Scripture says of him: 'The Lord swore and will not repent of it, "You are a priest forever"' – in so far Jesus has become the surety of a better covenant. Further, of the Levitical priests more and more were made priests because they were prevented from continuing permanently by death, whereas he has a priesthood which will never pass away, because he remains forever. For that very reason, it is in every possible way and for all time that he who is forever alive to make intercession for us can save those who come to God through him.

We needed such a high priest – one who is holy, one who has never hurt any man, one who is stainless, one who is different from sinners, one who has become higher than the heavens. He does not need, as the high priests do, daily first to offer sacrifices for his own sins and thereafter for the sins of the people. For he did this once and for all when he offered himself. For the law appointed as high priests men subject to weakness; but the word of the oath, which came after the law, appointed one who is a Son who is fully equipped to carry out his office forever.

THESE are the passages in which the writer to the Hebrews describes Jesus as *a priest after the order of Melchizedek*. Now, let us see just what he is trying to say when he uses that concept.

We must begin by understanding the general position from which he starts. He starts with the basic idea that *religion is access to God*. It was to make that access to God possible that two things existed. First, *the law*. The basic idea of the law is that, as long as men and women faithfully observe its commandments, they are in a position of friendship with God, and the door to God's presence is open to them. But they cannot keep the law, and therefore their fellowship with God and their access to his presence are interrupted. It was precisely to deal with that situation of estrangement that the second thing existed – *the priesthood and the whole sacrificial system*. The Latin word for *priest* is *pontifex*, which means a *bridge-builder*; the priest was someone whose function was to build a bridge between men and women and God by means of the sacrificial system. People broke the law; their fellowship with God was interrupted and their access to God was barred; by the offering of the correct sacrifice, that breach of the law was atoned for, and so the fellowship was restored and the barrier removed.

That was the theory. But, in practice, life showed that that was precisely what the priesthood and the sacrificial system could not do. There was no escaping the human estrangement from God which followed sin; and the problem was that not all the efforts of the priesthood and not all the sacrifices could restore that lost relationship. It is therefore the argument of the writer to the Hebrews that what is needed is a new and different priesthood and a new and effective sacrifice. He sees in Jesus Christ the only high priest who can open the way to God; and he calls the priesthood of Jesus a priesthood *after the order of Melchizedek.*

He got that idea from two passages in the Old Testament. The first was Psalm 110:4, where it is written:

The Lord has sworn and will not change his mind,
'You are a priest for ever after the order of Melchizedek.'

The second is Genesis 14:17–20, where the story of the original Melchizedek is told.

. . . the king of Sodom went out to meet him [Abram] at the Valley of Shaveh (that is, the King's Valley). And King Melchizedek of Salem brought out bread and wine; he was priest of God Most High. He blessed him and said, 'Blessed be Abram by God Most High, maker of heaven and earth; and blessed be God Most High, who has delivered your enemies into your hand!' And Abram gave him one-tenth of everything.

The writer to the Hebrews is here doing what any skilled Jewish Rabbi might do – following the Rabbinic method of interpretation. To understand that method, we must understand two things.

(1) To scholarly Jews, any passage of Scripture had *four* meanings to which they gave four different names. (a) First, there was *Peshat*, which is the literal and factual meaning.

(b) Second, there was *Remaz*, which is the suggested meaning. (c) Third, there was *Derush*, which is the meaning arrived at after long and careful investigation. (d) Fourth, there was *Sod*, which is the allegorical or inner meaning. To the Jews, the most important meaning by far was *Sod*, the inner meaning. They were not interested nearly so much in the factual meaning of a passage as in the allegorical and mystical meaning which could be extracted from it, even though it might have no connection whatever with the literal meaning. It was quite permissible, and in fact the regular practice, to take things right out of their context and read into them meanings which we would consider fantastic and quite unjustified. That is what the writer to the Hebrews is doing here.

(2) Second, it is essential to note that the Jewish interpreters considered themselves completely justified in arguing not only from the *utterances* but also from the *silences* of Scripture. An argument could be built not only on what Scripture said but also on what it did not say. In fact, the writer to the Hebrews bases his argument in this passage at least as much on what Scripture did not say about Melchizedek as on what it did.

Now, let us see how the quality of the priesthood after the order of Melchizedek differs from the quality of the ordinary Aaronic priesthood.

(1) *Melchizedek has no genealogy*; he is without father and without mother (Hebrews 7:3). Note straightaway that this is one of the arguments drawn from the *silence* of Scripture which does not provide Melchizedek with any genealogy. This was unusual for two reasons. (a) It is the reverse of the regular practice of Genesis. Genealogies are a feature of Genesis, where long lists of a man's ancestors constantly occur. But Melchizedek arrives on the scene, as it were, from nowhere. (b) Far more importantly, it is the reverse

of the rules which governed the Aaronic priesthood, which depended entirely on descent. Under Jewish law, a man could not under any circumstances become a priest unless he could produce a certificated pedigree going back to Aaron. Character and ability had nothing to do with it; the one essential was that pedigree. When the Jews came back to Jerusalem from exile, certain priestly families could not produce their genealogical records and were therefore debarred from the priesthood forever (Ezra 2:61–3; Nehemiah 7:63–5). On the other hand, if a man could produce a pedigree reaching back to Aaron, apart only from certain specified physical blemishes, nothing on earth could stop him from being a priest. Genealogy was literally everything.

So, the first difference between the two priesthoods was this: *the Aaronic priesthood depended on genealogical descent, while the priesthood of Melchizedek depended on personal qualification alone*. Melchizedek's priesthood was based on what *he was*, not on what *he had inherited*. As one scholar puts it, the difference was between a claim based on *legality* and a claim based on *personality*.

(2) Hebrews 7:1–3 collects further qualities about Melchizedek. The name *Melchizedek* literally means *King of Righteousness*. The word *Salem* means *peace*; therefore he was also *King of Peace*. We have seen that he has no genealogy. Again, the writer to the Hebrews draws on the silence of Scripture. We are told of no time when Melchizedek began or ended his priesthood; we are told of no time when he was born or died. Therefore, he had no beginning and has no end; and his priesthood lasts forever.

From this, we gather five great qualities in the priesthood of Melchizedek. (a) It is a priesthood of *righteousness*. (b) It is a priesthood of *peace*. (c) It is a *royal* priesthood, for Melchizedek was a king. (d) It is *personal and not inherited*, because he has no genealogy. (e) It is *eternal*, because he has no birth or death, and his priesthood has no beginning or end.

(3) Supposing all this is true, how can it be proved that the priesthood of Melchizedek is superior to the Aaronic? To prove this, the writer to the Hebrews seizes on two points in the Genesis story about Melchizedek.

First, there is the saying that *Abraham gave Melchizedek tithes of all.* The priests also exact payment of tithes (that is, payment of one-tenth of certain things); but there are two differences. The priests tithe their fellow Jews; and they tithe them as a result of legal requirements. But Melchizedek tithed Abraham, who had no racial connection with him whatsoever and was in fact the founder of the Jewish nation; further, he demanded the tithes not because the law gave him the right to do so but because of an unquestionable personal right. Obviously, that set him far above the ordinary priesthood.

Second, there is the saying that *Melchizedek blessed Abraham.* It is always the person who is superior who blesses the inferior; therefore Melchizedek was superior to Abraham although Abraham was the founder of the Jewish race and the unique recipient of the promises of God. That indeed gives Melchizedek the highest place above all others.

The scholar A. B. Bruce sums up the points in which Melchizedek was superior to the ordinary Levitical priesthood in this way. (a) He tithed Abraham and was therefore superior to him. Abraham was one of the patriarchs; the patriarchs are superior to their descendants, therefore Melchizedek is greater than the descendants of Abraham; the ordinary priests are the descendants of Abraham, therefore Melchizedek is greater than they. (b) Melchizedek is greater than the sons of Levi because they exacted tithes by legal right; but he did it as a right that he personally possessed and which had no human origin. (c) The Levites received tithes as mortals; he received them as one who lives forever (Hebrews 7:8). (d) Levi, to whom the Israelites paid tithes, may be said to have paid tithes to Melchizedek, because he was Abraham's grandson and was therefore in Abraham's body at the time Abraham paid tithes.

(4) Hebrews 7:11 onwards shows *where the superiority of the new priesthood lay*.

(a) *The very fact that a new priesthood was promised* (Hebrews 7:11) *shows that the old one was inadequate.* If the old priesthood had fulfilled the function of bringing people to the presence of God, there would have been no need for any other. Further, the introduction of the new priesthood was a revolution. According to the law, all priests must belong to the tribe of *Levi*; but Jesus was from the tribe of *Judah*. This shows that the whole old system was superseded. Something greater than the law had come.

(b) *The new priesthood was forever* (Hebrews 7:15–19). Under the old system, the priests died and there was no permanence; but now there had come a priest who lives forever.

(c) *The new priesthood was introduced by an oath of God.* Psalm 110:4 says: 'The Lord has sworn and will not change his mind, "You are a priest forever according to the order of Melchizedek".' Clearly, God does not take an oath lightly. He never introduced the ordinary priesthood like that. This was something new.

(d) *The new priest offered no sacrifice for himself* (Hebrews 7:27). The ordinary priest always had to make sacrifice for *his own* sin before he could do so for the sins of the people. But Jesus Christ, the new high priest, was sinless and needed no sacrifice for himself.

(e) *The new priest did not need endlessly to repeat sacrifices* (Hebrews 7:27). He made the one perfect sacrifice, which never needs to be made again because it has forever opened the way to the presence of God.

We now sum up briefly the ideas in the mind of the writer to the Hebrews when he thinks of Jesus in terms of the high priest after the order of Melchizedek. To make it clearer, we set out only the important and outstanding ideas without the minor points of detail.

(1) Jesus is the high priest, whose priesthood depends not on any genealogy but on himself alone.

(2) Jesus is the high priest who lives forever.

(3) Jesus is the high priest who himself is sinless and never needs to offer any sacrifice for his own sin.

(4) Jesus is the high priest who, in the offering of himself, made the perfect sacrifice which once and for all opened the way to God. No more sacrifice need be made.

Having seen the general ideas in the mind of the writer to the Hebrews concerning Jesus as a priest after the order of Melchizedek, we now turn to this passage in detail and study it in sections.

THE TRUE KING AND
THE TRUE PRIEST

Hebrews 7:1-3

> Now this Melchizedek was King of Salem and priest of the most high God. He met Abraham when he was returning from the smiting of the kings and blessed him, and Abraham set apart for him a tenth part of the spoils. In the first place, the interpretation of his own name means King of Righteousness and, in the second place, King of Salem means King of Peace. His father is never mentioned nor his mother; nor is there any record of his descent; there is no mention of the beginning of his days nor any of the end of his life; he is exactly like the Son of God; and he remains a priest forever.

As we have seen, the two passages on which the writer to the Hebrews founds his argument are Psalm 110:4 and Genesis 14:18–20. In the old Genesis story, Melchizedek is a strange and almost eerie figure. He arrives out of the blue; there is nothing about his life, his birth, his death or his descent. He simply arrives. He gives Abraham bread and wine, which to us, reading the passage in the light of what we know, sounds very sacramental. He blesses Abraham. And then he vanishes from the stage of history with the same unexplained suddenness as he arrived. There is little wonder that in the mystery of this story the writer to the Hebrews found a symbol of Christ.

From his name, Melchizedek was King of Righteousness, and from his realm King of Peace. The order is both significant and inevitable. *Righteousness must always come before peace*. Without righteousness, there can be no such thing as peace. As Paul has it in Romans 5:1: 'Therefore, since we are *justified* by faith, we have *peace* with God.' As he has it again in Romans 14:17: 'The kingdom of God is . . . *righteousness* and *peace* and joy.' The order is always the same – first righteousness and then peace.

It may well be said that all life is a search for peace, and also that people persist in looking for it in the wrong place.

(1) We look for peace in *escape*. But the trouble about escape is that it is always necessary to return. A. J. Gossip draws a picture of a woman whose home was a complete mess. She leaves her home one afternoon and goes to a cinema. For an hour or two, she escapes into the glamour and the luxury of the world of the film – and then she must go back home. It is escape all right – but there is the inevitable return. W. M. Macgregor tells of an old woman who lived in a terrible slum in Edinburgh called the Pans. Periodically, she would grow disgusted with the surroundings in which

she lived and would make a tour of her friends, extracting a small sum of money from each. With the proceeds, she would get helplessly drunk. When others remonstrated with her, she would answer: 'Do you grudge me my one chance to get out of the Pans with a sup of whisky?' Again it was escape – but she, too, had to return. It is always possible to find some kind of peace by the route of escape, but it is never a lasting peace. The great eighteenth-century man of letters Dr Samuel Johnson used to insist that everyone should have a hobby, for he held that people should have as many retreats for their minds as possible. But even there, there is the necessity to return. Escape is not wrong; sometimes it is necessary if health and sanity are to be preserved; but it is always something that only alleviates pain and is never a cure.

(2) There is the peace of *evasion*. Many people seek peace by refusing to face their problems: they push them to the back of their minds and seek to pull down the blind on them. There are two things to be said about that. The first is that no one ever solved a problem by refusing to face it. However much we evade it, it is still there. And problems are like diseases: the longer we refuse to take them seriously, the worse they get. We may well come to a stage when a disease is incurable and a problem insoluble. The second thing is maybe even more serious. Psychology tells us that there is a part of the mind which never stops thinking. With our conscious minds, we may be evading a problem; but our subconscious mind is teasing away at it. The thing is there like a piece of hidden shrapnel, a splinter of metal in the body; and it can ruin life. Far from bringing peace, evasion is most destructive of peace.

(3) There is the way of *compromise*. It is possible to arrive at some kind of peace by reaching some kind of compromise. It is in fact one of the most common methods of the world.

We can seek peace by toning down some principle or by an uneasy agreement in which neither party is fully satisfied. Kermit Eby says that, however long we compromise, the time comes when we must stand up and be counted if we want to sleep at night. Compromise means leaving the loose ends of things unsolved. Compromise, therefore, inevitably means tension, even if that tension is more or less hidden; tension inevitably means a gnawing worry; and therefore compromise really is the enemy of peace.

(4) There is the way of *righteousness*, or, to put it differently, the way of *the will of God*. There is no real peace for any of us until we have said: 'Your will be done.' But, once that has been said, peace floods the soul. It happened even to Jesus. He went into the Garden of Gethsemane with a soul under such tension that he sweated blood. In the garden, he accepted God's will and came out at peace. To take the way of righteousness, to accept God's will, is to remove the root cause of disquiet and find the way to lasting peace.

The writer to the Hebrews piles up words to show that Melchizedek has no descent. He does this to contrast the new priesthood of Jesus Christ with the old Aaronic priesthood. A Jew could not be a priest unless he could trace an unbroken descent from Aaron; but, if he could trace such a descent, nothing could stop him from being a priest. If a priest married and his bride-to-be was the daughter of a priest, she must produce her pedigree going back four generations; if she was not the daughter of a priest, she must produce her pedigree going back five generations. It is an odd and almost incredible fact that the whole Jewish priesthood was founded on genealogy. Personal qualities did not enter into it at all. But Jesus Christ was the true priest, not because of what he inherited but because of what he was.

Some of the words that the writer of Hebrews piles up here are amazing. He says that Jesus was *without descent* (*agenealogētos*). That is a word that, as far as we know, no Greek writer had ever used before. It may well be that, in his eagerness to stress the fact that Jesus' power did not depend on descent, he invented it. It is in all probability a new word to describe a new thing. He says that Melchizedek was without father (*apatōr*) and without mother (*amētōr*). These words are very interesting. They have certain uses in secular Greek. They are the regular description of the homeless and people with no family ties, and of people of low birth. They contemptuously dismiss people as having no ancestry. Further, *apatōr* has a technical legal use in the contemporary Greek of the papyri. It is the word which is used on legal documents, especially on birth certificates, for *father unknown* and, therefore, *illegitimate*. So, for instance, there is a papyrus which speaks of: 'Chairēmōn, *apatōr*, father unknown, whose mother is Thasēs.' It is amazing that the writer to the Hebrews took words like these to stress his meaning. The Christian writers had a strange way of redeeming words as well as redeeming men and women. No phrase seemed too strong to the writer to the Hebrews to insist upon the fact that Jesus' authority lay in himself and came from no one else.

THE GREATNESS OF MELCHIZEDEK

Hebrews 7:4–10

> Just see how great this man was – Abraham gave him the tenth part of the spoils of victory – and Abraham was no less than the founder of our nation. Now look at the difference – when the sons of Levi receive their priesthood, they receive an injunction laid down by the

law to exact tithes from the people. That is to say, they exact tithes from their own brothers, even although they are descendants of Abraham. But this man, whose descent is not traced through them at all, exacted tithes from Abraham and actually blessed the man who had received the promises. Beyond all argument, the lesser is blessed by the greater. Just so, in the one instance, it is a case of men who die receiving tithes; but, in this instance, it is the case of a man whom the evidence proves to live. Still further – if I may put it this way – through Abraham, Levi, too, the very man who receives the tithes, had tithes exacted from him, for he was in his father's body when Melchizedek met him.

THE writer to the Hebrews is here concerned to prove the superiority of the Melchizedek priesthood to the ordinary priesthood. He proceeds on the matter of tithes, because Abraham had given to Melchizedek a tenth part of the spoils of his victory. The law of tithes is laid down in Numbers 18:20–1. There, Aaron is told that the Levites will have no actual territory in the promised land set apart for them but that they are to receive a tenth part of everything for their services in the tabernacle. 'Then the Lord said to Aaron: "You shall have no allotment in their land, nor shall you have any share among them; I am your share and your possession among the Israelites. To the Levites I have given every tithe in Israel for a possession in return for the service that they perform, the service in the tent of meeting."'

So now, in a series of contrasts, the writer to the Hebrews works out the superiority of Melchizedek over the Levitical priests. He makes five different points. (1) The Levites receive tithes from the people, and that is a right that only they enjoy. Melchizedek received tithes from Abraham although he was not a member of the tribe of Levi. It could be argued that, while that put him on a level with the Levites, it does not prove that he was superior to them. So, our writer adds four other points. (2) The Levites tithe their fellow Israelites; Melchizedek was not an Israelite but a stranger; and it was no ordinary Israelite from whom he received tithes but from no less a person than Abraham, the founder of the nation. (3) It was due to a legal ruling that the Levites have the right to demand tithes; but Melchizedek received tithes because of what he was. He had such personal greatness that he needed no law to entitle him to receive tithes. (4) The Levites who receive tithes are mortal; but Melchizedek lives forever. (5) Finally, he produces a curious argument for which he apologizes before he states it. Levi was a direct descendant of Abraham and the only man legally entitled to receive tithes. Now, if he was a direct descendant of Abraham, it means that he was already in Abraham's body. Therefore, when Abraham paid tithes to Melchizedek, Levi also paid them, being included in Abraham's body, the final proof that Melchizedek was superior to him. It is an extremely odd argument; but it was, no doubt, convincing enough to those to whom it was addressed.

Strangely enough, this argument encapsulates the great truth that what people do affects their descendants. If they commit some sin, they may pass to their descendants either the tendency to that sin or some actual physical handicap because of it. If they develop excellence of character, they pass on a fine inheritance to those who come after. On the argument of the writer to the Hebrews, Levi was affected by what Abraham did. Within the intricacies of the strange Rabbinic argument, there remains the truth that we do not live for ourselves alone, but we transmit something of ourselves to those who follow after.

THE NEW PRIEST AND THE NEW WAY

Hebrews 7:11–20

> If, then, the desired effect could have been achieved by
> the Levitical priesthood – for it was on the basis of it
> that the people became a people of the law – what
> further need was there to set up another priest and to
> call him a priest after the order of Melchizedek, and not
> to call him a priest after the order of Aaron? Once the
> priesthood was altered, of necessity there follows an
> alteration of the law too, for the person of whom the
> statements are made belongs to another tribe altogether,
> from which no one ever served at the altar. It is obvious
> that it was from Judah that our Lord sprang, and, with
> regard to that tribe, Moses said nothing about priests.
> And certain things are still more abundantly clear – if a
> different priest is set up, a priest after the order of
> Melchizedek, a priest who has become so, not according
> to the law of a mere human injunction but according to
> the power of a life that is indestructible – for the witness
> of Scripture in regard to this is: 'You are a priest forever
> after the order of Melchizedek' – if all that is so, two
> things emerge. On the one hand, there emerges the
> cancellation of the previous injunction because of its
> own weakness and uselessness (for the law never
> achieved the effect which it was designed to produce)
> and, on the other hand, there emerges the introduction
> of a better hope through which we can come near to
> God.

As we read this passage, we have to remember the basic
idea of religion which never leaves the mind of the writer to
the Hebrews. To him, religion is access to God's presence as
friends, with nothing between us and him. The old Jewish
religion was designed to produce that fellowship in two ways.

First, there was obedience to the law. If people obeyed the law, they were the friends of God. Second, it was recognized that such perfect obedience could never be achieved; and so the sacrificial system came in. When someone was guilty of breaking the law, the appropriate sacrifice was supposed to put matters right. When the writer to the Hebrews says that the people became a people of the law on the basis of the Levitical priesthood, he means that, without the Levitical sacrifices to atone for breaches of it, the law would have been completely impossible. But, in fact, the system of Levitical sacrifices had proved ineffective to restore the lost fellowship between God and his people. So, a new priesthood was necessary – the priesthood after the order of Melchizedek.

He says that that priesthood differed from the old in that it was dependent not on merely human – *fleshly* is the word in the Greek – injunctions but on the power of a life that is indestructible. What he means is this. Every single regulation that governed the old priesthood had to do with the priest's physical body. To be a priest, he must be a pure descendant of Aaron. Even then, there were 142 physical blemishes which might disqualify him; some of them are detailed in Leviticus 21:16–23.

The ordination ceremony is outlined in Leviticus 8. (1) He was bathed in water so that he would be ceremonially clean. (2) He was clothed in the four priestly garments – the linen knee breeches, the long linen garment woven in one piece, the girdle round the breast, and the bonnet or turban. (3) He was anointed with oil. (4) He was touched on the tip of the right ear, his right thumb and his right big toe with the blood of certain sacrifices which had been made. Every single item in the ceremony affects the priest's body.

Once he was ordained, he had to observe a certain number of washings with water and anointings with oil; he also had to cut his hair in a certain way. From beginning to end, the Jewish priesthood was dependent on physical things. Character, ability and personality had nothing to do with it. But the new priesthood was dependent on *a life that is indestructible*. Christ's priesthood depended not on physical things but on what he was in himself. Here was a revolution: it was no longer outward ceremonies and observances that made a priest, but inward worth.

Further, there was another great change which had fundamental implications. The law was definite that all priests must belong to the tribe of *Levi*; they must be descendants of Aaron; but Jesus belonged to the tribe of *Judah*. Therefore, the very fact that he was the supreme priest meant that the law was cancelled; it was wiped out. The word used for cancellation is *athetēsis*; that is the word used for annulling a treaty, for cancelling a promise, for crossing someone's name off the register, for rendering a law or regulation inoperative. The whole paraphernalia of the ceremonial law was wiped out in the priesthood of Jesus.

Finally, Jesus can do what the old priesthood never could: he can give us access to God. How does he do that? What is it that keeps us from having access to God? (1) There is *fear*. As long as we are terrified of God, we can never be at home with him. Jesus came to show us the infinite, tender love of the God whose name is Father – and the awful fear is gone. We know now that God wants us to come home, not to punishment but to the welcome of his open arms. (2) There is *sin*. On his cross, Jesus made the perfect sacrifice which atones for sin. Fear is gone; sin is conquered; the way to God is open to all.

THE GREATER PRIESTHOOD

Hebrews 7:21–5

> And inasmuch as it happened with an oath – for the
> Levitical priests are made priests without an oath, but
> he with an oath, because Scripture says of him: 'The
> Lord swore and will not repent of it, "You are a priest
> forever"' – in so far Jesus has become the surety of a
> better covenant. Further, of the Levitical priests more
> and more were made priests because they were pre-
> vented from continuing permanently by death, whereas
> he has a priesthood which will never pass away, because
> he remains forever. For that very reason, it is in every
> possible way and for all time that he who is forever
> alive to make intercession for us can save those who
> come to God through him.

THE writer to the Hebrews is still accumulating his proofs
that the priesthood according to the order of Melchizedek,
the priesthood of Jesus, is superior to the old Levitical
priesthood. Here, he brings forward two other proofs.

First, he stresses the fact that the institution of the
priesthood after the order of Melchizedek was confirmed by
the oath of God while the ordinary priesthood was not. The
reference is to Psalm 110:4: '*The Lord has sworn* and will
not change his mind, "You are a priest for ever according to
the order of Melchizedek."' The very idea of God taking an
oath is startling. Long ago, the Jewish scholar Philo saw this.
He pointed out that the only reason for taking an oath is
because anyone's word can be disbelieved; and an oath is
taken to guarantee that a person's word is true. God never
needs to do that because it is impossible that his word should
ever be disbelieved. If, therefore, God ever confirms a statement by an oath, that statement must be of extraordinary

importance. So, it is possible that the ordinary priesthood can pass away; but the priesthood of Jesus Christ can never pass away, because God has sworn an oath that it will last forever.

Because this priesthood has been confirmed by an oath, Jesus is *the surety of a better covenant*. Let us remember that the function of the priest and of all religion is to open a way of access to God. Here, we come across the word *covenant*. We shall soon have to examine it in more detail. It is sufficient at the moment to say that a covenant is, in essence, an agreement between two people that, if one faithfully performs certain undertakings, the other will respond in a certain way.

There was an ancient covenant between Israel and God that, if the Israelites faithfully obeyed God's law, the way of access to his friendship would always be open to them. We see the nation entering into that covenant in Exodus 24:1–8. We see Moses taking the book of the law and reading it to the people; and we see the people responding with the words: 'All that the Lord has spoken we will do, and we will be obedient' (Exodus 24:7). The old agreement was based on obedience to the law; and the agreement could be kept open only while the priests continued to make sacrifice every time the law was broken.

Jesus is the surety of a new and a better covenant, a new kind of relationship between men and women and God. The difference is this: the old covenant was based on law and justice and obedience; the new covenant is based on love and on the perfect sacrifice of Jesus Christ. The old covenant was based on human achievement; the new covenant is based on God's love.

What does the writer to the Hebrews mean by saying that Jesus is the *surety* (*egguos*) of this new covenant? An *egguos* is one who gives security. It is used, for instance, of a person who guarantees someone else's overdraft at a bank; that person is surety that the money will be paid. It is used for someone who puts up bail for someone charged with an offence; that person guarantees that the one accused will appear at the trial. The *egguos* is one who guarantees that some undertaking will be honoured.

So, what the writer to the Hebrews means is this. Someone might say: 'How do you know that the old covenant is no longer operative? How do you know that access to God now depends not on our achievement of obedience but simply on the welcoming love of God?' The answer is: 'Jesus Christ guarantees that it is so. He is the surety who promises that God's love will be forthcoming, if only we take him at his word.' To put it in the simplest possible way, we must believe that, when we look at Jesus in all his love, we are seeing what God is like.

The writer to the Hebrews introduces a second proof of the superiority of the priesthood of Jesus. There was no permanency about the old priesthood. Those who were priests died and had to be replaced; but the priesthood of Jesus is forever. What really matters in this passage are the overtones and implications of the almost untranslatable words the writer uses.

He says that the priesthood of Jesus is one *that will never pass away* (*aparabatos*). *Aparabatos* is a legal word. It means *inviolable*. A judge lays down that his decision must remain *aparabatos*, *unalterable*. It means *non-transferable*. It describes something which belongs to one person and cannot ever be transferred to anyone else. Galen, the second-century Greek medical writer, uses it to describe absolute scientific law which can never be violated, the principles on which the very universe is built and holds together. So, the writer to the Hebrews says that the priesthood of Jesus is something which can never be taken from him, something that no one else can ever possess, something that is as lasting as the laws which hold the universe together. Jesus is and will always remain the only way to God.

The writer to the Hebrews uses another wonderful word about Jesus and says of him that *he remains forever* (*paramenein*). That verb has two characteristic senses. First, it means *to remain in office*. No one can ever take the office of Jesus from him; to all eternity, he remains the introducer of men and women to God. Second, it means *to remain in the capacity of a servant*. In the fourth century, Gregory of Nazianzus provided in his will that his daughters would *remain* (*paramenein*) with their mother as long as she was alive. They were to stay with her and be her help and support. The papyri talk of a girl who must *remain* (*paramenein*) in a shop for three years in order to discharge by her work a debt that she cannot pay. There is a papyrus contract which says that a boy who is being taken on as an apprentice must *remain* (*paramenein*) with his master for as many days extra as he has played truant. When the writer to the Hebrews says that Jesus *remains forever*, there is wrapped up in that phrase the amazing thought that *Jesus is forever at the service of men and women*. In eternity as he was in time, Jesus exists to be of service to all people. That is why he is the complete Saviour. On earth, he served men and women and gave his life for them; in heaven, he still exists to make intercession for them. He is the priest forever, the one who is forever opening the door to the friendship of God and is forever the great servant of all.

THE HIGH PRIEST WE NEED

Hebrews 7:26–8

> We needed such a high priest – one who is holy, one
> who has never hurt any man, one who is stainless, one
> who is different from sinners, one who has become
> higher than the heavens. He does not need, as the high
> priests do, daily first to offer sacrifices for his own sins
> and thereafter for the sins of the people. For he did this
> once and for all when he offered himself. For the law
> appointed as high priests men subject to weakness; but
> the word of the oath, which came after the law,
> appointed one who is a Son who is fully equipped to
> carry out his office forever.

STILL the writer to the Hebrews is filled with the thought of
Jesus as high priest. He begins this passage by using a series
of great words and phrases to describe him.

(1) He says that Jesus is *holy* (*hosios*). This word is used
of Jesus in Acts 2:27 and 13:35; it is used of the Lord in
Revelation 15:4 and 16:5; it is used of the Christian bishop in
Titus 1:8; it is used of the hands that must be presented to
God in prayer in 1 Timothy 2:8. Behind it, there is always
one special idea. It always describes those who faithfully do
their duty to God. It describes people not so much as they
appear before others but as they appear before God. *Hosios*
has in it the greatest of all goodnesses, the goodness which is
pure in the sight of God.

(2) He says that Jesus *never hurt anyone* (*akakos*). *Kakia*
is the Greek word for evil; and *akakos* describes someone
who is so cleansed of evil that only good remains. It describes
the effect an individual has upon other people. Sir Walter
Scott, the Scottish novelist, claimed for himself as a writer
that he never corrupted anyone's morals or unsettled anyone's

faith. Individuals who are described as *akakos* are so cleansed that their presence is like an antiseptic, and in their hearts there is nothing but the loving kindness of God.

(3) He says that Jesus is *stainless* (*amiantos*). *Amiantos* describes someone who is absolutely free from any of the blemishes which might make it impossible to draw near to God. The blemished victim cannot be offered to God; the defiled individual cannot approach him; but the one who is *amiantos* is fit to enter into God's presence.

(4) He says that Jesus is *different from sinners*. This phrase does not mean that Jesus was not really fully human. He was different from sinners in that, although he underwent every temptation, he conquered them all and emerged without sin. The difference between him and other men and women lies not in the fact that he was not fully human, but in the fact that he was the highest and best of all humanity.

(5) He says that Jesus *was made higher than the heavens*. In this phrase, he is thinking of the exaltation of Jesus. If the last phrase stresses the perfection of his humanity, this one stresses the perfection of his godhead. He who was truly one with us is also exalted to the right hand of God.

The writer to the Hebrews now introduces another aspect in which the priesthood of Jesus is far superior to the Levitical priesthood. Before the high priest could offer sacrifice for the sins of the people, he had first to offer sacrifice *for his own sins*, for he was a sinful man.

The writer is thinking particularly of the Day of Atonement. This was the great day when atonement was made for all the sins of the people, the day on which the high priest performed his supreme function. Usually, it was the only day in the year when he personally carried out the sacrifices. On ordinary days, they were left to the subordinate priests; but, on the Day of Atonement, the high priest himself officiated.

The very first item in the ritual of that day was a sacrifice for the sins of the high priest himself. He washed his hands and his feet; he put aside his gorgeous robes; he clothed himself in spotless white linen. A bullock that he had purchased with his own money was brought to him. He laid both hands on the bullock's head to transfer his sin to it; and he made confession in these words: 'Ah, Lord God, I have committed iniquity; I have transgressed; I have sinned – I and my house. O Lord, I beseech you, cover over the iniquities, the transgressions and the sins which I have committed, transgressed and sinned before you, I and my house.'

The greatest of all the Levitical sacrifices began with a sacrifice for the sins of the high priest. That was a sacrifice Jesus never needed to make, for he was without sin. The Levitical high priest was a sinful man offering animal sacrifices for sinful people; Jesus was the sinless Son of God offering himself for the sin of all. It was the law that had appointed the Levitical high priest; it was the oath of God that gave Jesus his office; and, because he was what he was, the sinless Son of God, he was equipped for his office as no human high priest could ever be.

Now the writer to the Hebrews does what he so often does. He puts down a marker to indicate the direction he is going to take. He says of Jesus that *he offered himself*. Two things were necessary in a sacrifice. There was the priest and there was the sacrifice. With long and intricate argument, the writer to the Hebrews has proved that Jesus was the perfect high priest; now he is going to move on to another thought. Not only was Jesus the perfect high priest; *he was also the perfect offering*. Jesus alone could open the way to God because he was the perfect high priest and he offered the one perfect sacrifice – himself.

There is much in this argument which is difficult for us to understand. It speaks and thinks in terms of ritual and ceremony long since forgotten; but one eternal thing remains. Men and women seek the presence of God; their sin has put up a barrier between them and God, but they are restless until they rest in God; and Jesus alone is the priest who can bring the offering that can open the way back to God.

THE WAY TO REALITY

Hebrews 8:1–6

> The pith of what we are saying is this – it is just such a high priest we possess, a priest who has taken his seat at the right hand of the throne of majesty in the heavens, a high priest who is a minister of the sanctuary and of the real tabernacle, which the Lord, and not man, founded. For every high priest is appointed to offer gifts and sacrifices. It is therefore necessary that he should have something which he might offer. If then he had been upon earth, he would not even have been a priest, for there already exist those who offer the gifts the law lays down, men whose service is but a shadowy outline of the heavenly order, just as Moses received instructions when he was about to complete the tabernacle – 'See', it says, 'that you do everything according to the pattern that was shown to you on the mountain.' But, as things are, he has obtained a more excellent ministry, in so far as he is also the mediator of a better covenant, a covenant which was enacted on the basis of superior promises.

THE writer to the Hebrews has finished describing the priesthood after the order of Melchizedek in all its glory. He has described it as the priesthood which is forever, without beginning and without end; the priesthood that God confirmed with an oath; the priesthood that is founded on personal greatness and not on any legal appointment or racial qualification; the priesthood which death cannot touch; the priesthood which is able to offer a sacrifice that never needs to be repeated; the priesthood which is so pure that it has no need to offer sacrifice for any sins of its own. Now he makes and underlines his great claim. 'It is', he says, 'a priest precisely like that that we have in Jesus.'

He goes on to say two things about Jesus. (1) He took his seat at the right hand of the throne of majesty in the heavens. That is the final proof of his *glory*. As words from Thomas Kelly's great hymn 'The head that once was crowned with thorns' express it:

> The highest place that heaven affords
> Is his, is his by right,
> The King of kings, and Lord of lords,
> And heaven's eternal light.

There can be no glory greater than that of the ascended and exalted Jesus. (2) He says that Jesus is a minister of the sanctuary. That is the proof of his *service*. He is unique both in majesty and in service.

Jesus never looked on majesty as something to be selfishly enjoyed. One of the greatest of the Roman emperors was Marcus Aurelius; as an administrator he was unsurpassed. He died at the age of 59, having worked himself to death in the service of his people. He was one of the Stoic saints. When chosen to succeed in due course to the imperial power, his biographer Capitolinus tells us, 'he was appalled rather than overjoyed, and when he was told to move to the private house of Hadrian, the Emperor, it was with reluctance that he departed from his mother's villa. And when the members of the household asked him why he was sorry to receive the royal adoption, he enumerated to them the toils which sovereignty involved.' Marcus Aurelius saw kingship in terms of service and not of majesty.

Jesus is the unique example of divine majesty and divine service combined. He knew that he had been given his supreme position, not jealously to guard it in splendid isolation, but rather to enable others to attain to it and to share it. In him, the supreme majesty and the supreme service met.

Now there enters into the picture a thought that was never far from the mind of the writer to the Hebrews. Religion to him, remember, was *access to God*; therefore the supreme function of any priest was to open the way to God for others. He removed the barriers between God and his people; he built a bridge across which men and women could go into the presence of God. But we could put this another way. Instead of talking about *access to God*, we might talk about *access to reality*. Every religious writer has to search for terms which the readers will understand. The message has to be presented in language and in thoughts which will make their point because they are familiar, or at least strike a chord in the reader's mind. The Greeks had a basic idea about the universe. They thought in terms of two worlds, the real and the unreal. They believed that this world of space and time was only a pale copy of the real world. That was the basic belief of Plato, the greatest of all the Greek thinkers. He believed in what he called *forms*. Somewhere there was a world where there existed the perfect forms of which everything in this world is an imperfect copy. Sometimes he called the forms *ideas*. Somewhere there is the idea of a chair of which all actual chairs are imperfect copies. Somewhere there is an idea of a horse of which all actual horses are inadequate reflections. The Greeks were fascinated by this conception of a real world of which this world is only a flickering, imperfect copy. In this world, we walk in shadows; somewhere there is reality. The great problem in life is how to pass from this world of shadows to the other world of realities. That is the idea of which the writer to the Hebrews makes use.

The earthly Temple is a pale copy of the real Temple of God; earthly worship is a remote reflection of real worship; the earthly priesthood is an inadequate shadow of the real priesthood. All these things point beyond themselves to the reality of which they are the shadows. The writer to the Hebrews even finds that idea in the Old Testament itself. When Moses had received from God instructions about the construction of the tabernacle and all its furnishings, God said to him: 'And see that you make them according to the pattern for them, which is being shown you on the mountain' (Exodus 25:40). God had shown Moses the real pattern of which all earthly worship is the ghost-like copy. So, the writer to the Hebrews says that the earthly priests have a service which is merely a *shadowy outline* of the heavenly order. For *shadowy outline*, he combines two Greek words: *hupodeigma*, which means *a specimen* or, still better, a sketch-plan, and *skia*, which means *a shadow*, a reflection, a phantom, a silhouette. The earthly priesthood is unreal and cannot lead people into reality; but Jesus *can*. We can say that Jesus leads us into the presence of God, or we can say that Jesus leads us into reality; it means the same thing. When the writer to the Hebrews spoke of *reality*, he was using language that his contemporaries used and understood.

In the highest that this world can offer, there is some imperfection. It never quite reaches what we know the thing might be. Nothing we ever experience or achieve here quite reaches the ideal that haunts us. The real world is beyond. As Robert Browning had it in 'Andrea del Sarto': 'A man's reach should exceed his grasp, or what's a heaven for?' Call it heaven, call it reality, call it the idea or the form, call it God – it is beyond.

As the writer to the Hebrews saw it, only Jesus can lead us out of the frustrating actuality into the all-satisfying real. So, he calls him the *mediator*, the *mesitēs*. *Mesitēs* comes from *mesos*, which, in this case, means *in the middle*. A *mesitēs* is, therefore, *one who stands in the middle between two people and brings them together*. When Job is desperately anxious that somehow he should be able to put his case to God, he cries out hopelessly: 'There is no umpire [*mesitēs*] between us' (Job 9:33). Paul calls Moses the *mesitēs* (Galatians 3:19) in that he was the one between, who brought the law from God to the people. In Athens in classical times, there was a body of men – all citizens in their sixtieth year – who could be called upon to act as mediators when there was a dispute between two citizens, and their first duty was to bring about a reconciliation. In Rome, there were *arbitri*. The judge settled points of law; but the *arbitri* settled matters of what was fair and just; and it was their duty to bring disputes to an end. Further, in legal Greek, a *mesitēs* was a *sponsor*, a *guarantor* or a *surety*. He put up bail for a friend who was on trial; he guaranteed a debt or an overdraft. The *mesitēs* was someone who was willing to pay a friend's debt to make things right again.

The *mesitēs* is the person who stands between and brings together two other parties in reconciliation. Jesus is our perfect *mesitēs*; he stands between us and God. He opens the way to reality and to God and is the only person who can bring about reconciliation between us and God, between the real and the unreal. In other words, Jesus is the only person who can bring us real life.

THE NEW RELATIONSHIP

Hebrews 8:7–13

> For, if the first covenant, which is so well known to
> you, had been faultless, there would have been no need
> to seek any place for a second one. It is to censure them
> that he says: 'Look you, the days are coming, says the
> Lord, when I will consummate a new covenant with the
> house of Israel and with the house of Judah. It will not
> be the same as the covenant which I made with their
> fathers, when I laid my hand on them to lead them forth
> from the land of Egypt; this must be so because they
> did not abide by my covenant, and I let them go their
> own way, says the Lord. It will be different because
> this is the covenant which I will make with the house
> of Israel after these days, says the Lord. I will put my
> laws into their mind and I will inscribe them upon their
> hearts. I will be to them all that a God should be to
> them, and they will be to me all that a people should be
> to me. And no one will teach his fellow citizen and no
> one will teach his brother, saying, "Know the Lord,"
> for all will know me, small and great alike, because I
> will graciously forgive their iniquities and I will not
> remember their sins any more.' In that he calls the
> covenant *new*, he has rendered the first covenant out of
> date; and that which is out of date and ageing into decay
> is near to final obliteration.

HERE, the writer to the Hebrews begins to deal with one of
the great biblical ideas – that of *a covenant*. In the Bible, the
Greek word that is always used for a covenant is *diathēkē* –
and there was a special reason for the choice of this rather
unusual word. Normally, a covenant is an agreement entered
into by two people. It is dependent on conditions on which
they mutually agree; and, if either should break the conditions,

the covenant becomes void. It is sometimes used in that simple sense in the Old Testament. For instance, it is used of the *treaty* that the Gibeonites wished to make with Joshua (Joshua 9:6), of the forbidden *covenant* with the Canaanites (Judges 2:2), and of David's *covenant* with Jonathan (1 Samuel 23:18). But its distinctive use is to describe the relationship between Israel and God. 'So be careful not to forget the *covenant* that the Lord your God made with you' (Deuteronomy 4:23). In the New Testament, the word is also used to describe the relationship between God and men and women.

But there is a strange point which requires explanation. For all normal uses, the Greek word for an agreement is *sunthēkē*, which is the word for a marriage covenant or bond and for an agreement between two states. Further, in all normal Greek, *diathēkē* means not an agreement but *a will*. Why should the New Testament use this word for a covenant? The reason is this: *sunthēkē* always describes an agreement entered into on equal terms. The parties to a *sunthēkē* are on the same level, and each can bargain with the other. But God and human beings do not meet on equal terms. In the biblical sense of a covenant, the whole approach comes from God. We cannot bargain with God; we cannot argue about the terms of the covenant; we can only accept or reject the offer that God makes.

The supreme example of such an agreement is *a will*. The conditions of a will are not made on equal terms. They are entirely one-sided, the terms being set by the person who made the will; and the other party cannot alter them but can only accept or refuse the inheritance offered.

That is why our relationship to God is described as a *diathēkē*, a covenant for the terms of which only one person is responsible. That relationship is offered to us solely on the initiative and the grace of God. As Philo said: 'It is fitting for God to give and for a wise man to receive.' When we use the word *covenant*, we must always remember that it does not mean that we have made a bargain with God on equal terms. It always means that the whole initiative is with God; the terms are his, and we cannot alter them in the slightest.

The ancient covenant, so well known to the Jews, was the one made with the people after the giving of the law. God graciously approached the people of Israel. He offered them a unique relationship to himself; but that relationship was entirely dependent on the keeping of the law. We see the Israelites accepting that condition in Exodus 24:1-8. The argument of the writer to the Hebrews is that that old covenant is done away with and that Jesus has brought a new relationship with God.

In this passage, we can distinguish certain marks of the new covenant which Jesus brought.

(1) The writer begins by pointing out that the idea of a new covenant is not something revolutionary. It is already there in Jeremiah 31:31-4, which he quotes in full. Further, the very fact that Scripture speaks of the new covenant shows that the old was not completely satisfactory. If it had been satisfactory, a new covenant would never have needed to be mentioned. Scripture looked to a new covenant and therefore itself indicated that the old covenant was not perfect.

(2) This covenant will not only be new; *it will be different in quality and in kind*. In Greek, there are two words for *new*. *Neos* describes a thing as being new in respect of time. It might be an exact copy of its predecessors; but, if it has been made after the others, it is *neos*. *Kainos* means not only new in relation to time, but also new in relation to quality. A thing

which is simply a reproduction of what went before may be *neos* – but it is not *kainos*. This covenant which Jesus introduces is *kainos*, not merely *neos*; it is different in quality from the old covenant. The writer to the Hebrews uses two words to describe the old covenant. He says that it is *gēraskōn*, which means not only *ageing* but *ageing into decay*. He says that it is near to *aphanismos*. *Aphanismos* is the word that is used for wiping out a city, obliterating an inscription or abolishing a law. So, the covenant which Jesus brings is new in quality and completely cancels the old.

(3) In what ways is this covenant new? *It is new in its scope.* It is going to include *the house of Israel and the house of Judah*. A millennium before this, in the days of Rehoboam, the kingdom had split apart, into Israel with ten of the tribes and Judah with the remaining two tribes; and these two sections had never come together again. The new covenant is going to unite that which has been divided; in it, the old enemies will be at one.

(4) *It is new in its universality.* Everyone, from the least to the greatest, would know God. That was something quite new. In the ordinary life of the Jews, there was a complete division. On the one hand, there were the Pharisees and the orthodox who kept the law; on the other hand, there were what were contemptuously called the people of the land, the ordinary people who did not fully observe the details of the ceremonial law. They were completely despised. It was forbidden for anyone in the first group to have any fellowship with them; to marry one's daughter to one of them was something not to be contemplated; it was forbidden to go on a journey with them; it was even forbidden, as far as it was possible, to have any trade or business dealings with them. To the rigid observers of the law, the ordinary people were beyond the pale. But, in the new covenant, these divisions

would no longer exist. All men and women, wise and simple, great and small, would know the Lord. The doors which had been shut were thrown wide open.

(5) There is one even more fundamental difference. The old covenant depended on obedience to an externally imposed law. *The new covenant is to be written upon human hearts and minds.* People would obey God not because of the terror of punishment, but because they loved him. They would obey him not because the law compelled them unwillingly to do so, but because the desire to obey him was written on their hearts.

(6) It will be a covenant *which will really bring about forgiveness.* See how that forgiveness is to come. *God said that he would be gracious to their iniquities and would forget their sins.* Now it is all from God. The new relationship is based entirely on his love. Under the old covenant, people could keep this relationship to God only by obeying the law; that is, by their own efforts. Now everything is dependent not on human efforts but solely on the grace of God. The new covenant puts men and women into relationship with a God who is still a God of justice but whose justice has been swallowed up in his love. The most tremendous thing about the new covenant is that it makes our relationship to God no longer dependent on our obedience but entirely dependent on God's love.

There is one thing left to say. In Jeremiah's words about the new covenant, there is no mention of sacrifice. It would seem that Jeremiah believed that, in the new age, sacrifice would be abolished as irrelevant; but the writer to the Hebrews can only think in terms of the sacrificial system, and very shortly he will go on to speak of Jesus as the perfect sacrifice, whose death alone made the new covenant possible.

THE GLORY OF THE TABERNACLE

Hebrews 9:1–5

> So, then, the first tabernacle, too, had its ordinances of worship and its holy place, which was an earthly symbol of the divine realities. For the first tabernacle was constructed and in it there was the lamp stand and the table with the shewbread, and it was called the holy place. Behind the second curtain, there was that part of the tabernacle which was called the Holy of Holies. It was approached by means of the golden altar of incense, and it had in it the ark of the covenant, which was covered all over with gold. In the ark, there was the golden pot with the manna and Aaron's rod which budded and the tables of the covenant. Above it, there were the cherubim of glory, overshadowing the mercy seat; but this is not the place to speak about all these things in detail.

THE writer to the Hebrews has just been thinking of Jesus as the one who leads us into reality. He has been using the idea that in this world we have only pale copies of what is truly real. The worship that we can offer is just a ghost-like shadow of the real worship which only Jesus, the real high priest, can offer. But even as he thinks of that, his mind goes back to the tabernacle (the tabernacle, remember, not the Temple). Lovingly he remembers its beauty; lovingly he lingers on its priceless possessions. And the thought in his mind is this: if earthly worship was as beautiful as this, what must the true worship be like? If all the loveliness of the tabernacle was only a shadow of reality, how surpassingly lovely the reality must be. He does not describe the tabernacle in detail; he only alludes to some of its treasures. This was all he needed to do because his readers knew its glories and had them fixed in their memories. But we do not know them; therefore, let us see what the beauty of the earthly tabernacle was like, always remembering that it was only a pale copy of reality.

The main description of the tabernacle in the wilderness is in Exodus 25–31 and 35–40. God said to Moses: 'Make me a sanctuary, so that I may dwell among them' (Exodus 25:8). It was constructed out of the free-will offerings of the people (Exodus 25:1–7), who gave with such lavish generosity that a halt had to be called to their giving (Exodus 36:5–7).

The court of the tabernacle was 150 feet long and 75 feet wide. It was surrounded by a curtain-like fence of fine, twined linen seven and a half feet high. The white linen stood for the wall of holiness that surrounds the presence of God. The curtain was supported by twenty pillars on the north and south sides, and by ten on the east and west sides; and the pillars were set in sockets of brass and had tops of silver. There was only one gate. It was on the east side, and it was thirty feet wide and seven and a half feet high. It was made of fine, twined linen and with blue, purple and scarlet yarns. In the court, there were two things. There was the *bronze altar*, seven and a half feet square and four and a half feet high and made of acacia wood sheathed in brass. Its top was a bronze grating on which the sacrifice was laid; and it had four horns to which the offering was bound. There was *the laver*. The laver was made from the brass mirrors of the women (glass mirrors did not exist at that time), but its dimensions are not given. The priests bathed themselves in the water in it before they carried out their sacred duties.

The tabernacle itself was constructed of forty-eight acacia beams, fifteen feet high and two feet three inches wide. They were overlaid with pure gold and rested in sockets of silver. They were bound together by outside connecting rods and by a wooden tie-beam which ran through their centre. The tabernacle was divided into two parts. The first – two-thirds of the whole – was *the holy place*; the inner part – one-third of the whole – a cube fifteen feet on each side, was *the Holy of Holies*. The curtain which hung in front of *the holy place* was supported on five brass pillars and made of fine linen worked in blue, purple and scarlet.

The holy place contained three things. (1) There was *the golden lamp stand*. It stood on the south side; it was beaten out of a single piece of solid gold; the lamps were fed with pure olive oil, and were always lit. (2) On the north side stood *the table of the shewbread*. It was made of acacia wood covered with gold; it was three feet long, one and a half feet wide and two feet three inches high. Every Sabbath, twelve loaves made of the finest flour were laid on it, in two rows of six. Only the priests could eat these loaves when they were removed. They were changed every Sabbath. (3) There was *the altar of incense*. It was of acacia wood sheathed in gold; it was one and a half feet square and three feet high. On it, incense, symbolizing the prayers of the people rising to God, was burned every morning and evening.

In front of *the Holy of Holies*, there was *the veil*, which was made of fine, twined linen, embroidered in scarlet and purple and blue, and with the cherubim upon it. Into *the Holy of Holies*, no one but the high priest might enter – and he only once a year, on the Day of Atonement, and only after the most elaborate preparations. Within the Holy of Holies stood *the ark of the covenant*. It contained three things – the golden pot of the manna (see Exodus 16:31–3), Aaron's rod that budded (see Numbers 17:8), and the tables of the law. It was made of acacia wood sheathed outside and lined inside with gold. It was three feet nine inches long, two feet three inches wide, and two feet three inches high. Its lid was called *the mercy-seat*. On the mercy-seat, there were two cherubim of solid gold with overarching wings. It was there that the very presence of God rested, for he had said: 'There I will meet you, and from above the mercy-seat, from between the two cherubim that are on the ark of the covenant' (Exodus 25:22).

It was of all this beauty that the writer to the Hebrews was thinking – and yet it was only a shadow of reality. In his mind, there was another thing of which he was to speak again: the ordinary Israelite could come only to the gate of the tabernacle court; the priests and the Levites might enter the court; the priests alone might enter the holy place; and none but the high priest might enter the Holy of Holies. There was beauty, but it was a beauty in which the ordinary people were barred from the inner presence of God. Jesus Christ took the barrier away and opened wide the way to God's presence for everyone.

THE ONLY ENTRY TO
THE PRESENCE OF GOD

Hebrews 9:6–10

> Since these preparations have been made, the priests continually enter into the first tabernacle as they perform the various acts of worship. But into the second tabernacle the high priest alone enters, and that once a year and not without blood, which he offers for himself and for the errors of the people. By this the Holy Spirit is showing that the way into the Holy Place was not yet opened up so long as the first tabernacle stood. Now the first tabernacle stands for this present age, and according to its services sacrifices are offered which cannot perfect the conscience of the worshipper but which, since they are based on food and drink and

various kinds of washings, are human regulations, laid
down until the time of the new order should come.

ONLY the high priest could enter into the Holy of Holies, and
then only on *the Day of Atonement*. It is of the ceremonies of
that day that the writer to the Hebrews is thinking here. He
did not need to describe them to his readers, because they
knew them. To them, they were the most sacred religious
ceremonies in all the world. If we are to understand the
thought of the writer to the Hebrews, we must have a picture
of them in our minds. The main description is in Leviticus
16.

First, we must ask, what was the idea behind the Day of
Atonement? As we have seen, the relationship between Israel
and God was a covenant relationship. Sin on Israel's part
broke that relationship, and the whole system of sacrifice
existed to make atonement for sin and to restore the broken
relationship. But what if there were some sins still not atoned
for? What if there were some sins of which people were not
conscious? What if, by some chance, the altar itself had
become defiled? That is to say, what if the sacrificial system
was not performing the function it should?

The summary of the Day of Atonement is given in
Leviticus 16:33:

> He shall make atonement for the sanctuary, and he shall
> make atonement for the tent of meeting and for the altar,
> and he shall make atonement for the priests and for all
> the people of the assembly.

It was one great comprehensive act of atonement for all sin.
It was a splendid day in which all things and all people were
cleansed, so that the relationship between Israel and God
should continue unbroken. To that end, it was a day of humiliation. 'You shall deny yourselves' (Leviticus 16:29). It was

not a *feast* but a *fast*. The whole nation fasted all day, even the children; and really devout Jews prepared themselves for it by fasting for ten days beforehand. The Day of Atonement comes ten days after the start of the Jewish New Year, about the beginning of September in our calendar. It was the greatest of all days in the life of the high priest.

Let us see what happened. Very early in the morning, the high priest cleansed himself by washing. He put on his gorgeous robes of office, worn only on that day. There were the white linen breeches and the long white undergarment reaching down to the feet, woven in one piece. There was *the robe of the ephod*. It was dark blue and was a long robe which at its foot had a fringe of blue, purple and scarlet tassels made in the form of pomegranates, interspersed with an equal number of little golden bells. Over this robe, he put *the ephod* itself. The ephod was probably a kind of linen tunic, embroidered in scarlet and purple and gold, with an elaborate girdle. On its shoulders were two onyx stones. The names of six of the tribes were engraved on one stone and six on the other. On the tunic was *the breastplate*, a span, that is about nine inches, square. On it were twelve precious stones with the names of the twelve tribes engraved upon them. So, the high priest carried the people to God on his shoulders and on his heart. In the breastplate, there was the *Urim and the Thummim*, which means *lights and perfections* (Exodus 28:30). What exactly the Urim and the Thummim was is not known. It is known that the high priest consulted it when he wished to know the will of God. It may be that it was a precious diamond inscribed with the consonants IHWH which are the consonants of *Yahweh*, the name of God. On his head, the high priest put the tall *mitre*, of fine linen; and on the mitre there was a gold plate bound by a band of blue ribbon, and on the plate were the words: 'Holiness unto the Lord.' It is easy to imagine what a dazzling figure the high priest must have appeared on this his greatest of all days.

The high priest began by doing the things that were done every day. He burned the morning incense, made the morning sacrifice, and attended to the trimming of the lamps on the seven-branched lamp stand. Then came the first part of the special ritual of the day. Still dressed in his gorgeous robes, he sacrificed a bullock and seven lambs and one ram (Numbers 29:7). Then he removed his gorgeous robes, cleansed himself again in water, and dressed himself in the simple purity of white linen. There was brought to him a bullock bought with his own resources. He placed his hands on its head and, standing there in the full sight of the people, confessed his own sin and the sin of his family:

> Ah, Lord God, I have committed iniquity; I have transgressed; I have sinned – I and my house. O Lord, I entreat thee, cover over [atone for] the iniquities, the transgressions and the sins which I have committed, transgressed and sinned before you, I and my house, even as it is written in the law of Moses, thy servant, 'For in that day, he will cover over [atone] for you to make you clean. From all your transgressions before the Lord, you shall be cleansed.'

For the time being, the bullock was left in front of the altar. And then followed one of the unique ceremonies of the Day of Atonement. Two goats were standing by, and beside the goats was an urn with two lots in it. One lot was marked *For Yahweh*; the other was marked *For Azazel*, which is the phrase the Authorized Version translates as *the Scapegoat*. The lots were drawn and laid one on the head of each goat. A tongue-shaped piece of scarlet was tied to the horn of the scapegoat. And for the moment the goats were left. Then the high priest turned to the bullock which was beside the altar and killed it. Its throat was slit and the blood caught in a basin by a priest. The basin was kept in motion so that the blood would not coagulate, for soon it was to be used. Then came the first of the great moments. The high priest took coals from the altar and put them in a censer; he took incense and put it in a special dish; and then he walked into the Holy of Holies to burn incense in the very presence of God. It was laid down that he must not stay too long 'lest he put Israel in terror'. The people literally watched with bated breath; and, when he came out from the presence of God still alive, there went up a sigh of relief like a gust of wind.

When the high priest came out from the Holy of Holies, he took the basin of the bullock's blood, went back into the Holy of Holies and sprinkled it seven times up and seven times down. He came out, killed the goat that was marked *For Yahweh*, with its blood re-entered the Holy of Holies and sprinkled again. Then he came out and mixed together the blood of the bullock and the goat and seven times sprinkled the horns of the altar of the incense and the altar itself. What remained of the blood was laid at the foot of the altar of the burnt offering. Thus the Holy of Holies and the altar were cleansed by blood from any defilement that might be on them.

Then came the most vivid ceremony. The scapegoat was brought forward. The high priest laid his hands on it and confessed his own sin and the sin of the people; and the goat was led out into the desert, 'into a land not inhabited', laden with the sins of the people, and there it was killed.

The priest turned to the slain bullock and goat and prepared them for sacrifice. Still in his linen garments, he read Scripture – Leviticus 16, 23:27–32, and repeated by heart Numbers 29:7–11. He then prayed for the priesthood and the people.

Once more, he cleansed himself in water and dressed himself again in his gorgeous robes. He sacrificed first a young goat for the sins of the people; then he made the normal evening sacrifice; then he sacrificed the already prepared parts of the bullock and the goat. Then once again he cleansed himself, took off his robes, and put on the white linen; and for the fourth and last time he entered the Holy of Holies to remove the censer of incense which still burned there. Once again he cleansed himself in water; once again he put on his vivid robes; then he burned the evening offering of incense, trimmed the lamps on the golden lamp stand, and his work was done. In the evening, he held a feast because he had been in the presence of God and had come out alive.

That was the ritual of the Day of Atonement, the day designed to cleanse all things and all people from sin. That was the picture in the mind of the writer to the Hebrews – and he was to make much of it. But there were certain things of which he was thinking at the time.

Every year, this ceremony had to be gone through again. Everyone but the high priest was barred from the presence, and even he entered in terror. The cleansing was a purely external one by baths of water. The sacrifice was that of bulls and goats and animal blood. The whole thing failed because such things cannot atone for sin. In it all, the writer to the Hebrews sees a pale copy of the reality, a ghostly pattern of the one true sacrifice – the sacrifice of Christ. It was a noble ritual, a thing of dignity and beauty; but it was only a shadow which could not succeed in its purpose. The only priest and the only sacrifice which can open the way to God for *all* men and women is Jesus Christ.

THE SACRIFICE WHICH OPENS
THE WAY TO GOD

Hebrews 9:11–14

> But when Christ arrived upon the scene, a high priest
> of the good things which are to come, by means of a
> tabernacle which was greater and better able to produce
> the results for which it was meant, a tabernacle not
> made by the hands of men – that is, a tabernacle which
> did not belong to this world order – and not by the
> blood of goats and bullocks but by his own blood, he
> entered once and for all into the holy place because
> he had secured for us an eternal redemption. For if
> the blood of goats and bulls and the ashes of a heifer
> could by sprinkling cleanse those that were unclean
> so that their bodies became pure, how much more will
> the blood of Christ, who through the eternal Spirit
> offered himself spotless to God, cleanse your con-
> science so that you will be able to leave the deeds that
> make for death in order to become the servants of the
> living God?

WHEN we try to understand this passage, we must remember
three things which are basic to the thought of the writer to
the Hebrews. (1) Religion is access to God. Its function is to
bring people into God's presence. (2) This is a world of pale
shadows and imperfect copies; beyond is the world of
realities. The function of all worship is to bring people
into contact with the eternal realities. That was what the
worship of the tabernacle was meant to do; but the earthly
tabernacle and its worship are pale copies of the real
tabernacle and its worship; and only the real tabernacle and
the real worship can give access to reality. (3) There can be
no religion without sacrifice. Purity is a costly thing; access

to God demands purity; somehow human sin must be atoned for and uncleanness cleansed. With these ideas in his mind, the writer to the Hebrews goes on to show that Jesus is the only high priest who brings a sacrifice that can open the way to God, and that that sacrifice is himself.

To begin with, he refers to certain of the great sacrifices which the Jews were in the habit of making under the old covenant with God. (1) There was the sacrifice of *bullocks* and of *goats*. In this, he is referring to two of the great sacrifices on the Day of Atonement – of the bullock which the high priest offered for his own sins, and of the scapegoat which was led away to the wilderness bearing the sins of the people (Leviticus 16:15, 21–2). (2) There was the sacrifice of the *red heifer*. This strange ritual is described in Numbers 19. Under Jewish ceremonial law, if someone touched a dead body, that person was unclean. Such people were barred from the worship of God, and everything and everyone they touched also became unclean. To deal with this, there was a prescribed method of cleansing. A red heifer was slaughtered outside the camp. The priest sprinkled the blood of the heifer in front of the tabernacle seven times. The body of the beast was then burned, together with cedar and hyssop and a piece of red cloth. The resulting ashes were placed outside the camp in a clean place and constituted a purification for sin. This ritual must have been very ancient, for both its origin and its meaning are extremely obscure. The Jews themselves told that, once, a Gentile questioned Rabbi Jochanan ben Zakkai on the meaning of this rite, declaring that it sounded like pure superstition. The Rabbi's answer was that it had been appointed by the Holy One and that no one should inquire into his reasons, but the matter should be left there without explanation. In any event, the fact remains that it was one of the great Jewish rites.

The writer to the Hebrews tells of these sacrifices and then declares that the sacrifice that Jesus brings is far greater and far more effective. We must first ask what he means by the greater and more effective tabernacle not made with hands. That is a question to which no one can give an answer which is beyond dispute. But the ancient scholars nearly all took it in one way and said that this new tabernacle which brought people into the very presence of God was nothing other than the body of Jesus. It would be another way of saying what John said: 'Whoever has seen me has seen the Father' (John 14:9). The worship of the ancient tabernacle was designed to bring people into the presence of God, but only in the most shadowy and imperfect way. The coming of Jesus really brought men and women into the presence of God, because in him God entered this world of space and time in a human form, and to see Jesus is to see what God is like.

The great superiority of the sacrifice Jesus brought lay in three things. (1) The ancient sacrifices cleansed the body from ceremonial uncleanness; the sacrifice of Jesus cleansed the soul. We must always remember this – in theory, all sacrifice cleansed from transgressions of the ritual law; it did not cleanse from presumptuous or high-handed sins. Take the case of the red heifer. It was not *moral* uncleanness that its sacrifice wiped out but the ceremonial uncleanness that resulted from touching a dead body. An individual's body might be clean ceremonially, and yet the heart of that person might be torn with remorse. A person might feel able to enter the tabernacle and yet at the same time be far away from the presence of God. The sacrifice of Jesus takes the load of guilt from people's *consciences*. The animal sacrifices of the old covenant might well leave them estranged from God; the sacrifice of Jesus shows us a God whose arms are always outstretched and in whose heart is only love.

(2) The sacrifice of Jesus brought eternal redemption. The idea was that human beings were under the dominion of sin; and, just as the purchase price had to be paid to free individuals from slavery, so the purchase price had to be paid to free us from sin.

(3) The sacrifice of Christ enabled people to leave the deeds of death and to become the servants of the living God. That is to say, he did not only win forgiveness for past sin, he enabled men and women in the future to live godly lives. The sacrifice of Jesus was not only the paying of a debt; it was the giving of a victory. What Jesus did puts us right with God, and what he does enables us to stay right with God. The act of the cross brings the love of God to us in a way that takes our terror of him away; the presence of the living Christ brings the power of God to us so that we can win a daily victory over sin.

The New Testament scholar B. F. Westcott outlines four ways in which Jesus' sacrifice of himself differs from the animal sacrifices of the old covenant.

(1) The sacrifice of Jesus was *voluntary*. The animal's life was taken from it; Jesus *gave* his life. He willingly laid it down for his friends.

(2) The sacrifice of Jesus was *spontaneous*. Animal sacrifice was entirely *the product of law*; the sacrifice of Jesus was entirely *the product of love*. We pay our debts in business dealings because we have to; we give gifts to our loved ones because we want to. It was not law but love that lay behind the sacrifice of Christ.

(3) The sacrifice of Jesus was *rational*. The animal victim did not know what was happening; Jesus all the time knew what he was doing. He died, not as an ignorant victim caught up in circumstances over which he had no control and did not understand, but with eyes wide open.

(4) The sacrifice of Jesus was *moral*. Animal sacrifice was mechanical; but Jesus' sacrifice was made through *the eternal Spirit*. What happened on Calvary was not a matter of prescribed ritual, mechanically carried out; it was a matter of Jesus obeying the will of God for the sake of men and women. Behind it, there was not the mechanism of law but the choice of love.

THE ONLY WAY IN WHICH SINS CAN BE FORGIVEN

Hebrews 9:15-22

It is through him that there emerges a new covenant between God and man; and the purpose behind this new covenant is that those who have been called might receive the eternal inheritance which has been promised to them; but this could happen only after a death had taken place, the purpose of which was to rescue them from the consequences of the transgressions which had been committed under the conditions of the old covenant. For where there is a will, it is necessary that there should be evidence of the death of the testator before the will is valid. It is in the case of dead people that a will is confirmed, since surely it cannot be operative when the testator is still alive. That is why even the first covenant was not inaugurated without blood. For, after every commandment which the law lays down had been announced by Moses to all the people, he took the blood of calves and goats, together with water and scarlet and hyssop, and sprinkled the book itself and all the people. And as he did so, he said: 'This is the blood of the covenant whose conditions God commanded you to observe.' In like manner, he

sprinkled with blood the tabernacle also and all the
instruments used in its worship. Under the conditions
which the law lays down, it is true to say that almost
everything is cleansed by blood. Without the shedding
of blood, there is no forgiveness.

THIS is one of the most difficult passages in the whole letter,
although it would not be difficult to those who were first to
read the letter, for its methods of argument and expression
and categories of thought would be familiar to them.

As we have seen, the idea of the *covenant* is basic to the
thought of the writer, by which he meant a relationship
between God and human beings. The first covenant was
dependent on people keeping the law; as soon as they broke
the law, the covenant became ineffective. Let us remember
that, to our writer, *religion means access to God*. Therefore,
the basic meaning of the *new covenant*, which Jesus inaugurated, is that men and women should have access to God
or, to put it another way, have *fellowship* with him. But here
is the difficulty. People come to the new covenant already
stained with the sins committed under the old covenant, for
which the old sacrificial system was powerless to atone. So,
the writer to the Hebrews has a tremendous thought and says
that the sacrifice of Jesus Christ is effective retrospectively.
That is to say, it wipes out the sins committed under the old
covenant and inaugurates the fellowship promised under the
new covenant.

All that seems very complicated; but, behind it, there are
two great eternal truths. First, the sacrifice of Jesus gains
forgiveness for past sins. We ought to be punished for what
we have done, and to be shut out from God; but, because of
what Jesus did, the debt is wiped out, the breaking of the law
is forgiven and the barrier is taken away. Second, the sacrifice
of Jesus opens a new life for the future. It opens the way to

fellowship with God. The God whom our sins had made a stranger, the sacrifice of Christ has made a friend. Because of what he did, the burden of the past is rolled away, and life becomes life with God.

It is the next step in the argument which seems to us a fantastic way in which to argue. The question in the mind of the writer is why this new relationship with God should involve the *death* of Christ. He answers it in two ways.

(1) His first answer is – to us almost incredibly – founded on nothing other than a play on words. We have seen that the use of the word *diathēkē* in the sense of *covenant* is characteristically Christian, and that its normal secular use was in the sense of *will* or *testament*. Up to verse 16, the writer to the Hebrews has been using *diathēkē* in the normal Christian sense of *covenant*; then, suddenly and without warning or explanation, he switches to the sense of *will*. Now, a *will* does not become operative until the testator dies; so the writer to the Hebrews says that no *diathēkē*, *will*, can be operative until the death of the testator, so that the new *diathēkē*, *covenant*, cannot become operative apart from the death of Christ. That is a merely verbal argument and is quite unconvincing to our way of thinking; but it must be remembered that basing an argument on a play between two meanings of a word was a favourite method of the Alexandrian scholars in the time when this letter was written. In fact, in the days when the letter to the Hebrews was written, this very argument would have been considered an exceedingly clever piece of exposition.

(2) His second answer goes back to the Hebrew sacrificial system and to Leviticus 17:11: 'For the life of the flesh is in the blood; and I have given it to you on the altar for making atonement for your lives; *for, as life, it is the blood that makes atonement.*' 'Without the shedding of blood there can be no

atonement for sin,' was actually a well-known Jewish principle. So, the writer to the Hebrews goes back to the inauguration of the first covenant under Moses, the occasion when the people accepted the law as the condition of their special relationship with God. We are told how sacrifice was made and how Moses 'took half of the blood and put it in basins, and half of the blood he dashed against the altar' (Exodus 24:6). After the book of the law had been read and the people had signified their acceptance of it, Moses 'took the blood and dashed it on the people, and said, "See the blood of the covenant that the Lord has made with you in accordance with all these words"' (Exodus 24:8). It is true that the memory of the writer to the Hebrews, in citing that passage, is not strictly accurate. He introduces calves and goats and scarlet and hyssop which come from the ritual of the Day of Atonement, and he talks about the sprinkling of the tabernacle, which at that time had not yet been built; but the reason is that these things are so much in his mind. His basic idea is that there can be no cleansing and no confirmation of any covenant without the shedding of blood. *Why* that should be so, he does not need to know. Scripture says it is so, and that is enough for him. The probable reason is that, for the Jews, blood is life, and life is the most precious thing in the world; and people must offer that most precious thing to God.

All that goes back to a ritual which is only of historical interest. But, behind it, there is an eternal principle – *forgiveness is a costly thing. Human forgiveness* is costly. A son or a daughter may go wrong and a father or a mother may forgive; but that forgiveness brings tears, whiteness to the hair, lines to the face, a cutting anguish and then a long, dull ache to the heart. It does not cost nothing. *Divine forgiveness* is costly. God is love – but he is also *holiness*. He, least of all, can break the great moral laws on which the universe is built. Sin must have its punishment, or the very structure of life disintegrates. And God alone can pay the terrible price that is necessary before we can be forgiven. Forgiveness is never a case of saying: 'It's all right; it doesn't matter.' It is the most costly thing in the world. Without the shedding of the heart's blood, there can be no forgiveness of sins. Nothing brings people to their senses with such arresting violence as seeing the effect of their sin on someone who loves them in this world or on the God who loves them forever, and to say to themselves: 'It cost *that* to forgive *my* sin.' Where there is forgiveness, someone must be crucified.

THE PERFECT PURIFICATION

Hebrews 9:23–8

So, then, if it was necessary that the things which are copies of the heavenly realities should be cleansed by processes like these, it is necessary that the heavenly realities themselves should be cleansed by finer sacrifices than those of which we have been thinking. It is not into a man-made sanctuary that Christ has entered – that would be a mere symbol of the things which are real. It is into heaven itself that he entered, now to appear on our behalf before the presence of God. It is not that he has to offer himself repeatedly, as the high priest year by year enters into the holy place with a blood that is not his own. Were that so, he would have had to suffer again and again since the world was founded. But now, as things are, once and for all, at the end of the ages, he has appeared with his sacrifice of himself so that our sins should be cancelled. And, just as it is laid down for men to die once and for all and then to

face the judgment, so Christ, after being once and for
all sacrificed to bear the burden of the sins of many,
will appear a second time, not this time to deal with sin,
but for the salvation of those who are waiting for him.

THE writer to the Hebrews, still thinking of the supreme
effectiveness of the sacrifice which Jesus made, begins with
a flight of thought which, even for such an adventurous writer,
is amazing. Let us remember again the letter's basic thought
that the worship of this world is a pale copy of the real
worship. The writer to the Hebrews says that, in this world,
the Levitical sacrifices were designed to purify the means of
worship. For instance, the sacrifices of the Day of Atonement
purified the tabernacle and the altar and the holy place. Now
he goes on to say that the work of Christ purifies *not only
earth but also heaven*. He has the tremendous thought of a
kind of cosmic redemption that purified the whole universe,
seen and unseen.

So, he goes on to stress again the way in which the work
and the sacrifice of Christ are supreme.

(1) Christ did not enter a holy place that had been specially
created for worship; he entered into the presence of God. We
are to think of Christianity not in terms of church membership
but in terms of intimate fellowship with God.

(2) Christ entered into the presence of God not only for
his own sake but also for ours. It was to open the way for us
and to plead our cause. In Christ, there is the greatest paradox
in the world, the paradox of the greatest glory and the greatest
service, the paradox of one for whom the world exists and
who exists for the world, the paradox of the eternal king and
the eternal servant.

(3) The sacrifice of Christ never needs to be made again.
Year after year, the ritual of the Day of Atonement had to go
on, and the things that blocked the road to God had to be

atoned for; but, through Christ's sacrifice, the road to God is always open. Men and women were always sinners and always will be, but that does not mean that Christ must go on offering himself again and again. The road is open once and for all. We can draw a faint analogy of that. For a long time, a particular surgical operation may be impossible. Then some surgeon finds a way round the difficulties. From that day, that same road is open to all surgeons. We may put it this way: nothing need ever be added to what Jesus Christ has done to keep open the way to God's love for sinning humanity.

Finally, the writer to the Hebrews draws a parallel between human life and the life of Christ.

(1) Human beings die, and then comes the judgment. That itself was a shock to the Greeks, for they tended to believe that death was final. It was a belief expressed in the writings of the greatest Greek poets and dramatists. 'When earth once drinks the blood of a man,' said Aeschylus, 'there is death once and for all and there is no resurrection.' Euripides said: 'It cannot be the dead to light shall come.' 'For the one loss is this that never mortal maketh good again the life of man – though wealth may be re-won.' Homer makes Achilles say when he reaches the realm of the dead: 'Rather would I live upon the soil as the hireling of another, with a landless man whose livelihood was small, than bear sway among all the dead who are no more.' The Greek poet Mimnermus writes with a kind of despair:

> O Golden love, what life, what joy but thine?
> Come death, when thou art gone, and make an end!

There is a simple Greek epitaph:

> Farewell, tomb of Melitē; the best of women lies here,
> who loved her loving husband, Onesimus; you were
> most excellent, wherefore he longs for you after your

> death, for you were the best of wives. Farewell you too,
> dearest husband, only love my children.

As G. Lowes Dickinson, who wrote about the life of the ancient Greeks, points out, in the Greek, the first and the last word of that epitaph is 'Farewell!' Death was the end. When Tacitus wrote the tribute of biography to the great Agricola, all he could finish with was an 'if'.

> If there be any habitation for the spirits of just men, if,
> as the sages will have it, great souls perish not with the
> body, may you rest in peace.

'If' is the only word. Marcus Aurelius can say that when a person dies and the individual spark goes back to be lost in God, all that is left is 'dust, ashes, bones and stench'. The significant thing about this passage from Hebrews is its basic assumption that people will rise again. That is part of the certainty of the Christian creed; and the basic warning is that they rise to judgment.

(2) With Christ, it is different – he dies and rises and comes again, and he comes not to be judged but to judge. The early Church never forgot the hope of the second coming. That hope throbbed through their belief. But, for the unbeliever, that coming day was a day of terror. As the Book of Enoch describes the day of the Lord, before Christ came: 'For all you who are sinners there is no salvation, but upon you all will come destruction and a curse' (1 Enoch 5:6). In some way, the consummation must come. If in that day Christ comes as a friend, it can be only a day of glory; if he comes as a stranger or as one whom we have regarded as an enemy, it can be only a day of judgment. We may look to the end of things with joyous expectation or with shuddering terror. What makes the difference is how our hearts are with Christ.

THE ONLY TRUE SACRIFICE

Hebrews 10:1–10

Because the law is only a pale shadow of the blessings which are to come and not a real image of these things, it can never really fit for the fellowship of God those who seek to draw near to his presence with the sacrifices which have to be brought year by year and which go on forever. For if these sacrifices could achieve that, would they not have stopped being brought because the worshipper had been once and for all brought into a state of purity and no longer had any consciousness of sin? So far from that, in them there is a year-by-year reminder of sin. For it is impossible for the blood of bulls and goats to take away sin. That is why he says as he enters the world: 'You did not desire sacrifice and offering; it is a body you have prepared for me. You took no pleasure in whole burnt offerings and in sin offerings. So then I said: "So then I come – in the roll of the book it is written of me – to do, O God, your will." ' At the beginning of this passage, he says: 'You did not desire sacrifices and offerings and whole burnt offerings and sin offerings and you took no pleasure in them,' and it is such offerings as these that the law prescribes. Then he went on to say: 'Behold, I come to do your will.' He abolishes the kind of offerings referred to in the first quotation in order to establish the kind of offering referred to in the second. It is by this way of 'the will' that we have been purified through the once-and-for-all offering of the body of Christ.

To the writer to the Hebrews, the whole business of sacrifice was only a pale copy of what real worship ought to be. The purpose of religion was to bring people into a close relationship with God, and that is what these sacrifices could never do. The best that they could do was to provide a distant and occasional contact with God. He uses two words to indicate what he means. He says that these things are a *pale shadow*. The word he uses is *skia*, the Greek for *a shadow*, and it means a vague reflection, a mere silhouette, a form without reality. He says that they do not give a *real image*. The word he uses is *eikōn*, which means a *complete representation, a detailed reproduction*. It actually means a *portrait*, and would mean a *photograph*, if there had been such a thing in those days. In effect, he is saying: 'Without Christ, you cannot get beyond the shadows of God.'

He brings proof. Year by year, the sacrifices of the tabernacle and especially of the Day of Atonement go on. An effective thing does not need to be done again; the very fact of the repetition of these sacrifices is the final proof that they are *not* purifying human souls and *not* giving full and uninterrupted access to God. Our writer goes further: he says that all they are is *a reminder of sin*. Far from purifying people, they remind them that they are not purified and that their sins still stand between them and God.

Let us take an analogy. Someone is ill. A bottle of medicine is prescribed. If that medicine brings about a cure, the sight of the bottle will be a reminder and that person will say: 'That is what gave me back my health.' On the other hand, if the medicine is ineffective, the bottle will be a reminder that the person is still ill and that the recommended cure was useless.

So, the writer to the Hebrews says with prophetic vehemence: 'The sacrifice of animals is powerless to bring about purification and give access to God. All that such sacrifices can do is to remind people that they are uncured sinners and

that the barrier of their sin stands between them and God.'
Far from erasing the sin, they underline it.

The only effective sacrifice is the sacrifice of Jesus Christ.
To make his point and to explain what is in his mind, the
writer of Hebrews takes a quotation from Psalm 40:6–9. The
passage runs:

> Sacrifice and offering you do not desire,
> but you have given me an open ear.
> Burnt-offering and sin-offering you have not required.
> Then I said, 'Here I am;
> in the scroll of the book it is written of me.
> I delight to do your will, O my God.'

The writer to the Hebrews quotes it differently, and in the
second line he has:

> but a body you have prepared for me.

The explanation is that he was quoting not from the original
Hebrew but from the Septuagint, the Greek translation of the
Old Testament. In about 270 BC, the task of translating the
Old Testament into Greek was begun in Alexandria in Egypt.
Obviously, far more people in the ancient world read Greek
than Hebrew. It is very likely that the writer to the Hebrews
did not know any Hebrew at all, and therefore it is the
Septuagint that he uses. In any event, the meaning of the two
phrases is the same. 'You have given me an open ear' means:
'You have so touched me that everything I hear I obey.' It is
the obedient ear of which the psalmist is thinking. 'A body
you have prepared for me' really means: 'You created me so
that in my body and with my body I should do your will.' In
essence, the meaning is the same.

The writer to the Hebrews has taken the words of the psalm
and put them into the mouth of Jesus. What they say is that

God wants not animal sacrifices but *obedience to his will*. In its essence, sacrifice was a noble thing. It meant taking something that was dear and giving it to God in order to show love. But, human nature being what it is, it was easy for the idea to degenerate and for sacrifice to be thought of as a way of buying God's forgiveness.

The writer to the Hebrews was not saying anything new when he said that obedience was the only true sacrifice. Long before him, the prophets had seen how sacrifice had degenerated and had told the people that what God wanted was not the blood and the flesh of animals but the obedience of an individual's life. That is precisely one of the noblest thoughts of the Old Testament writers.

> And Samuel said, 'Has the Lord as great delight in burnt-offerings and sacrifices, as in obedience to the voice of the Lord? Surely, to obey is better than sacrifice, and to heed than the fat of rams.' (1 Samuel 15:22)

> Offer to God a sacrifice of thanksgiving,
> and pay your vows to the Most High. (Psalm 50:14)

> For you have no delight in sacrifice;
> if I were to give a burnt-offering, you would not be
>   pleased.
> The sacrifice acceptable to God is a broken spirit;
> a broken and contrite heart, O God, you will not despise.
> (Psalm 51:16–17)

> For I desire steadfast love and not sacrifice, the knowledge of God, rather than burnt-offerings. (Hosea 6:6)

> What to me is the multitude of your sacrifices? says the Lord; I have had enough of burnt-offerings of rams and

the fat of fed beasts; I do not delight in the blood of
bulls, or of lambs, or of goats . . . bringing offerings is
futile; incense is an abomination to me . . . When you
stretch out your hands, I will hide my eyes from you;
even though you make many prayers, I will not listen;
your hands are full of blood . . . cease to do evil, learn
to do good. (Isaiah 1:11–17)

'With what shall I come before the Lord, and bow
myself before God on high? Shall I come before him
with burnt-offerings, with calves a year old? Will the
Lord be pleased with thousands of rams, with tens of
thousands of rivers of oil? Shall I give my firstborn for
my transgression, the fruit of my body for the sin of my
soul?' He has told you, O mortal, what is good; and
what does the Lord require of you but to do justice, and
to love kindness, and to walk humbly with your God.
(Micah 6:6–8)

Always there had been voices crying out for God that the
only sacrifice was the sacrifice of obedience. Nothing but
obedience could open the way to God; disobedience set up a
barrier that no animal sacrifice could ever take away. Jesus
was the perfect sacrifice *because he perfectly did God's will.*
He took himself and said to God: 'Do with me as you will.'
He brought to God on behalf of men and women what no one
had been able to bring – the perfect obedience, that was the
perfect sacrifice.

If we are ever to have fellowship with God, obedience is
the only way. What we could not offer, Jesus offered. In his
perfect humanity, he offered the perfect sacrifice of the perfect
obedience. Through that, the way was once and for all opened
up for us.

THE FINALITY OF CHRIST

Hebrews 10:11–18

> Again, every priest stands every day engaged upon his service; he stands offering the same sacrifices over and over again, and they are sacrifices of such a kind that they can never take away sins. But he offered one single sacrifice for sin and then took his seat forever at the right hand of God, and for the future he waits until his enemies are made the footstool of his feet. For by one offering and for all time he perfectly gave us that cleansing we need to enter into the presence of God. And to this the Holy Spirit is our witness, for after he has said: 'This is the covenant I will make with them after these days, says the Lord. I will put my laws upon their hearts; and I will write them upon their minds,' he goes on to say: 'And I will not remember any more their sins and their breaches of the law.' Now, where there is forgiveness of these things, a sacrifice for sin is no longer necessary.

ONCE again, the writer to the Hebrews is drawing a series of implicit contrasts between the sacrifice that Jesus offered and the animal sacrifices that the priests offer.

(1) He stresses *the achievement of Jesus*. The sacrifice of Jesus was made once and is effective forever; the animal sacrifices of the priests must be made over and over again, and even then they are not effective in any real way. Every day, as long as the Temple stood, the following sacrifices had to be carried out (Numbers 28:3–8). Every morning and every evening, a male lamb, one year old, without spot and blemish, was offered as a *burnt offering*. Along with it, there was offered a *food offering*, which consisted of one-tenth of an ephah of fine flour mixed with a quarter of a hin of pure oil –

that is, a measure of flour equivalent in volume to around three litres and about one litre of oil. There was also a *drink offering*, which consisted of a quarter of a hin of wine. Added to that, there was *the daily food offering of the high priest*; it consisted of one-tenth of an ephah of fine flour, mixed with oil, and baked in a flat pan; half was offered in the morning and half in the evening. In addition, there was an offering of *incense* before these offerings in the morning and after them in the evening. There was a kind of priestly treadmill of sacrifice. In his commentary, James Moffatt speaks of 'the levitical drudges' who, day in day out, kept offering these sacrifices. There was no end to this process, and it left people still conscious of their sin and alienated from God.

In contrast, Jesus had made a sacrifice that neither could nor needed to be repeated.

(a) It *could* not be repeated. There is something un-repeatable about any great work. It is possible to repeat the popular tunes of the day endlessly; to a great extent, one echoes another. But it is not possible to repeat the Fifth or the Ninth Symphony of Beethoven; no one else will ever write anything like them. It is possible to repeat the kind of poetry that is written in sentimental magazines and on Christmas cards, but not to repeat the blank verse of Shakespeare's plays or the poetic metre of Homer's *Iliad*. These things stand alone. Certain things can be repeated; but all works of genius have a certain unrepeatable quality. It is so with the sacrifice of Christ. It is unique; it is one of these masterpieces which can never be done again.

(b) It *need* not be repeated. For one thing, *the sacrifice of Jesus perfectly shows the love of God*. In that life of service and in that death of love, there stands fully displayed the heart of God. Looking at Jesus, we can say: 'That is what

God is like.' What is more, *the life and death of Jesus was an act of perfect obedience and, therefore, the only perfect sacrifice*. All Scripture, at its deepest, declares that the only sacrifice God desires is obedience; and, in the life and death of Jesus, that is precisely the sacrifice that God received. Perfection cannot be improved upon. In Jesus, there is at one and the same time the perfect revelation of God and the perfect offering of obedience. Therefore, his sacrifice cannot and need not ever be made again. The priests must go on with their weary routine of animal sacrifice; but the sacrifice of Christ was made once and for all.

(2) He stresses *the exaltation of Jesus*. It is with care that he chooses his words. The priests *stand* offering sacrifice; Christ *sits* at the right hand of God. Theirs is the position of a servant; his is the position of a monarch. Jesus is the King who has come home, his task accomplished and his victory won. There is a *wholeness* about the life of Jesus to which we perhaps ought to give more thought. His life is incomplete without his death; his death is incomplete without his resurrection; his resurrection is incomplete without his return to glory. It is the same Jesus who lived and died and rose again and is at the right hand of God. He is not simply a saint who lived a lovely life, not simply a martyr who died a heroic death, not simply a risen figure who returned to keep company with his friends. He is the Lord of glory. His life is like a panelled tapestry; to look at one panel is to see only a little bit of the story. The tapestry must be looked at as a whole before the full greatness is disclosed.

(3) He stresses *the final triumph of Jesus*. He awaits the final overcoming of his enemies; in the end, there must come a universe in which he is supreme. How that will come is not ours to know; but it may be that this final overcoming will consist not in the extinction of his enemies but in their

submission to his love. It is not so much the power but the love of God which must conquer in the end.

Finally, as is his habit, the writer to the Hebrews clinches his argument with a quotation from Scripture. Jeremiah, speaking of the new covenant which will not be imposed from outside but which will be written on the heart, ends: 'I will . . . remember their sin no more' (Jeremiah 31:34). Because of Jesus, the barrier of sin is taken away forever.

THE MEANING OF CHRIST FOR US

Hebrews 10:19–25

Since then, brothers, in virtue of what the blood of Jesus has done for us, we can confidently enter into the Holy Place by the new and living way which Jesus inaugurated for us through the veil – that is, through his flesh – and, since we have a great high priest who is over the house of God, let us approach the presence of God with a heart wherein the truth dwells and with the full conviction of faith, with our hearts so sprinkled that they are cleansed from all consciousness of evil and with our bodies washed with pure water. Let us hold fast to the undeviating hope of our creed, for we can rely absolutely on him who made the promises; and let us put our minds to the task of spurring each other on in love and fine deeds. Let us not abandon our meeting together – as some habitually do – but let us encourage one another, and all the more so as we see the day approaching.

THE writer to the Hebrews now comes to the practical implication of all that he has been saying. From theology, he turns to practical exhortation. He is one of the most profound theologians in the New Testament, but all his theology is governed by the pastoral instinct. He does not think merely for the thrill of intellectual satisfaction, but only that he may more forcibly appeal to men and women to enter into the presence of God.

He begins by saying three things about Jesus.

(1) *Jesus is the living way to the presence of God.* We enter into the presence of God by means of the veil, that is, by the flesh of Jesus. That is a difficult thought, but what he means is this. In front of the Holy of Holies in the tabernacle, there hung the veil to screen off the presence of God. For anyone to enter into that presence, the veil would have to be torn apart. Jesus' flesh is what veiled his godhead. Charles Wesley, in his great hymn 'Hark the herald angels sing', made this appeal:

Veiled in flesh the godhead see.

It was when the flesh of Christ was torn upon the cross that people really saw God. All his life showed God; but it was on the cross that God's love really was revealed. As the tearing of the tabernacle veil opened the way to the presence of God, so the tearing of the flesh of Christ revealed the full greatness of his love and opened up the way to him.

(2) *Jesus is the high priest over God's house in the heavens.* As we have seen so often, the function of the priest was to build a bridge between the people and God. This means that Jesus not only shows us the way to God but also, when we get there, introduces us to his very presence. Someone might be able to direct a tourist who asks the way to Buckingham Palace and yet be very far from having the right to take that person into the presence of the Queen; but Jesus can take us the whole way.

(3) *Jesus is the one person who can really cleanse.* In the priestly ritual, the holy things were cleansed by being

sprinkled with the blood of the sacrifices. Again and again, the high priest bathed himself in the brass basin of clear water. But these things were ineffective to remove the real pollution of sin. Only Jesus can really cleanse people. His is no external purification; by his presence and his Spirit, he cleanses their innermost thoughts and desires until they are really clean.

From this, the writer to the Hebrews goes on to urge three things.

(1) *Let us approach the presence of God.* That is to say, let us never forget the duty of worship. It is given to everyone to live in two worlds – this world of space and time, and the world of eternal things. Our danger is that we become so involved in this world that we forget the other. As the day begins, as the day ends and repeatedly throughout the day's activities, we should turn aside, if only for a moment, and enter God's presence. We all carry with us our own secret shrine, but so many of us forget to enter it. As Matthew Arnold wrote in his poem 'Absence':

> But each day brings its petty dust
> Our soon-choked souls to fill;
> And we forget because we must,
> And not because we will.

(2) *Let us hold fast to our creed.* That is to say, let us never lose our grip of what we believe. The cynical voices may try to take our faith away; the materialists and their arguments may try to make us forget God; the events of life may conspire to shake our faith. The writer Robert Louis Stevenson said that he so believed in the ultimate decency of things that if he woke up in hell he would still believe in it; and we must have a grip on the faith that nothing can loosen.

(3) *Let us put our minds to the task of taking thought for others.* That is to say, let us remember that we are Christians

not only for our own sake but also for the sake of others. No one ever achieved personal salvation by devoting all time and energy to that purpose; but many have saved their souls by being so concerned for others that they forgot that they had their own souls to save. It is easy to drift into a kind of selfish Christianity; but a selfish Christianity is a contradiction in terms.

But the writer to the Hebrews goes on to outline our duty to others in the most practical way. He sees that duty extend in three directions.

(1) *We must encourage one another to noble living*. We can do that best by setting a good example. We can do it by reminding others of their traditions, their privileges and their responsibilities when they are likely to forget them. It has been said that a saint is someone in whom Christ stands revealed; we can seek always to encourage others to goodness by showing them Christ. We may remember how the dying soldier looked up at Florence Nightingale as she helped the wounded of the Crimean War, and murmured: 'You're Christ to me.'

(2) *We must worship together*. There were some among those to whom the writer of the Hebrews was writing who had abandoned the habit of meeting together. It is still possible for some to think that they are Christians and yet abandon the habit of worshipping with God's people in God's house on God's day. They may try to be what James Moffatt called 'a pious particle', a Christian in isolation. Moffatt distinguishes three reasons which keep people from worshipping with their fellow Christians.

(a) They may not go to church because of *fear*. They may be ashamed to be seen going to church. They may live or work among people who laugh at churchgoers. They may have friends who have no time for that kind of thing and may fear their criticism and contempt. They may, therefore, try to be secret disciples; but it has been well said that this is impossible because either 'the discipleship kills the secrecy or the secrecy kills the discipleship'. It would be a good thing if we remembered that, apart from anything else, to go to church is to demonstrate where our loyalty lies. Even if the sermon is poor and the worship uninspiring, the church service still gives us the chance to show to others what side we are on.

(b) They may not go because they are *over-particular*. They may shrink from contact with people who are 'not like them'. There are congregations which are as much clubs as they are churches. There may be congregations where a form of social snobbery is practised. We must never forget that there is no such thing as a 'common' person in the sight of God. It was for *all*, not only for the 'respectable' classes, that Christ died.

(c) They may not go because of *conceit*. They may believe that they do not need the Church or that they are intellectually beyond the standard of preaching there. Social snobbery is bad, but spiritual and intellectual snobbery is worse. The wisest person is a fool in the sight of God; and the strongest person is weak in the moment of temptation. There is no one who can live the Christian life and neglect the fellowship of the Church. If people feel that they can do so, let them remember that they come to church not only *to get* but also *to give*. If they think that the Church has faults, it is their duty to come in and help to correct them.

(3) *We must encourage one another.* One of the highest of human duties is that of encouragement. There is a regulation in the Royal Navy which says: 'No officer shall speak discouragingly to another officer in the discharge of duties.' Eliphaz unwillingly paid Job a great tribute. As Moffatt translates it: 'Your words have kept men on their feet' (Job

4:4). The writer J. M. Barrie somewhere wrote to Cynthia Asquith, the wife of the Liberal statesman: 'Your first instinct is always to telegraph to Jones the nice thing Brown said about him to Robinson. You have sown a lot of happiness that way.' It is easy to laugh at people's ideals, to pour cold water on their enthusiasm, to discourage them. The world is full of discouragers; we have a Christian duty to encourage one another. So many times, words of praise or thanks or appreciation or cheer have kept people on their feet. Blessed are those who speak such words.

Finally, the writer to the Hebrews says that our Christian duty to each other is all the more pressing because the time is short. The day is approaching. He is thinking of the second coming of Christ when things as we know them will be ended. The early Church lived in that expectation. Whether or not we still do, we must realize that none of us knows when the summons to rise and go will come to us also. In the time we have, it is our duty to do all the good we can to all the people we can in all the ways we can.

THE THREAT AT THE HEART OF THINGS

Hebrews 10:26–31

> For, if we deliberately sin after we have received full knowledge of the truth, no sacrifice for sin is left. All that we can expect is to wait in terror for judgment and for that flaming wrath which will consume the adversaries of God. Anyone who regards the law of Moses as a dead letter dies without pity on the evidence of two or three witnesses. Of how much worse punishment, do you think, that man will be deemed worthy who has trampled underfoot the Son of God, who has failed to regard the blood of the new covenant, with

which he was made fit for God's presence, as a sacred thing, and who has insulted the Spirit through whom God's grace comes to us? For we know who it was who said: 'Vengeance belongs to me; it is I who will repay,' and again: 'The Lord will judge his people.' It is a terrifying thing to fall into the hands of the living God.

EVERY now and again, the writer to the Hebrews speaks with a sternness that is almost without parallel in the New Testament. Few writers have such a sense of the sheer horror of sin. In this passage, his thoughts are going back to the grim instruction in Deuteronomy 17:2–7. It is there laid down that, if any person shall be proved to have gone after strange gods and to have worshipped them, 'you shall bring out to your gates that man or that woman who has committed this crime and you shall stone the man or woman to death. On the evidence of two or three witnesses the death sentence shall be executed; a person must not be put to death on the evidence of only one witness. The hands of the witnesses shall be the first raised against the person, to execute the death penalty, and afterwards the hands of all the people. So you shall purge the evil from your midst.'

The writer to the Hebrews has this horror of sin for two reasons.

First, he lived in a day when the Church had been under attack and would be under attack again. Its greatest danger was from the possible evil living and rejection of the faith by its members. A church in such circumstances could not afford to carry members who were a bad advertisement for the Christian faith. Its members must be loyal or nothing. That is still true. The Anglican pacifist priest Dick Sheppard spent much of his life preaching in the open air to people who were either hostile or indifferent to the Church. From their questions and their arguments and their criticisms, he said that he had learned that 'the greatest handicap the Church has is the unsatisfactory lives of professing Christians'. Christians who lead such unsatisfactory lives undermine the very foundations of the Church.

Second, the writer to the Hebrews was sure that sin had become doubly serious because of the new knowledge of God and of God's will which Jesus had brought. One of the early theologians wrote a kind of catechism. He ended by asking what happens if people disregard the offer of Jesus Christ. His answer was that condemnation must necessarily follow, 'and so much the more *because you have read this book*'. The greater the knowledge, the greater the sin. The conviction of the writer to the Hebrews was that, if under the old law rejection of the faith was a terrible thing, it had become doubly terrible now that Christ had come.

He gives us three definitions of sin.

(1) *Sin is to trample Christ underfoot.* It is not mere rebelliousness against law; it is the wounding of love. It is possible to stand almost any physical attack; the thing that brings submission is a broken heart. It is told that, in the days of the Nazi terror, there was a man in Germany who was arrested, tried, tortured and put into a concentration camp. He faced it all with gallantry and emerged upright and unbroken. Then, by accident, he discovered who it was who had produced the information against him – it was his own son. The discovery broke him, and he died. Attack by an enemy he could bear; attack by one whom he loved killed him. When Caesar was about to be murdered, he faced his assassins with almost disdainful courage. But when he saw the hand of his friend Brutus raised to strike, he wrapped his head in his mantle and died. Once Christ had come, the

awfulness of sin lay not in its breaking of the law but in its trampling of the love of Christ underfoot.

(2) *Sin is the failure to see the sacredness of sacred things.* Nothing produces a shudder like sacrilege. The writer to the Hebrews says in effect: 'Look at what has been done for you; look at the shed blood and the broken body of Christ; look at what your new relationship to God cost; can you treat it as if it did not matter? Don't you see what a sacred thing it is?' Sin is the failure to realize the sacredness of that sacrifice upon the cross.

(3) *Sin is the insult to the Holy Spirit*. The Holy Spirit speaks within us, telling us what is right and wrong, seeking to check us when we are on the way to sin and to spur us on when we are drifting into lethargy. To disregard these voices is to insult the Spirit and to grieve the heart of God.

All through this, one thing comes out. Sin is not disobedience to an impersonal law; it is the wrecking of a personal relationship and the wounding of the heart of the God whose name is Father.

The writer to the Hebrews finishes his appeal with a threat. He quotes Deuteronomy 32:35-6, where the sternness of God is clearly seen. At the heart of Christianity, there is always a threat. To remove that threat is to diminish the effectiveness of the faith. Ultimately, it is not the same for the good and the bad alike. No one can evade the fact that, in the end, judgment comes.

THE DANGER OF DRIFTING

Hebrews 10:32-9

> Remember the former days. Remember how, after you
> had been enlightened, you had to go through a hard

struggle of suffering, partly because you yourselves were held up to insult and involved in affliction and partly because you had become partners with people whose life was like that. For you gave your sympathy to those in prison; you accepted the pillaging of your goods with joy; for you knew that you yourselves hold a possession which is better and which lasts. Do not throw away your confidence, for it is a confidence that has a great reward. You need fortitude so that, after you have done the will of God, you may receive the promise. For, in a short time, a very short time, 'He who is to come will come and he will not delay. And my just man shall live by faith; but, if he shrinks back, my soul will not find pleasure in him.' We are not men to shrink back from things and so to come to disaster, but we are men of a faith which will enable us to possess our souls.

THERE had been a time when those to whom this letter was written had experienced fierce opposition to their beliefs. When they had first become Christians, they had known persecution and plundering of their goods; and they had learned what it was to become involved with those who were under suspicion and unpopular. They had met that situation with gallantry and with honour; and now, when they were in danger of drifting away, the writer to the Hebrews reminds them of their former loyalty.

It is a truth of life that, in many ways, it is easier to stand adversity than to stand prosperity. Comfort has ruined far more people than trouble ever did. The classic example is what happened to the armies of Hannibal.

Hannibal of Carthage was the one general who had routed the Roman legions. But winter came, and the campaign had to be put on hold. Hannibal wintered his troops in Capua which he had captured, a city of luxury. And one winter in

Capua did what the Roman legions had not succeeded in doing. The luxury so sapped the morale of the Carthaginian troops that, when the spring came and the campaign was resumed, they were unable to stand up to the Romans.

Comfort had ruined them when struggle had only toughened them. That is often true of Christian life. It is often the case that people are able to meet the great hour of testing and of trial with honour; and yet they allow the times of plain sailing to sap their strength and weaken their faith.

The appeal of the writer to the Hebrews is one that could be made to us all. In effect, he says: 'Be what you were at your best.' If only we were always at our best, life would be very different. Christianity does not demand the impossible; but, if we were always as honest, as kind, as courageous and as courteous as we can be, life would be transformed.

To be like that, we need certain things.

(1) *We need always to keep our hope in sight.* Athletes will make a great effort because the goal beckons. They will submit to the discipline of training because of the end in view. If life is only a day-to-day matter of routine things, we may well sink into a policy of drifting; but, if we are on the way to heaven's crown, our efforts must always be the very best we can offer.

(2) *We need fortitude.* Perseverance is one of the great unromantic virtues. Most people can start well, and almost everyone can keep going intermittently. To everyone at some time or other, strength and inspiration come so that we rise above things as if we had wings; in the moment of the great effort, everyone can run and not be weary; but the greatest gift of all is to walk on steadily and not to faint.

(3) *We need the memory of the end.* The writer to the Hebrews quotes a passage from Habakkuk 2:3. The prophet tells his people that, if they hold fast to their loyalty, God

will see them through their present situation. The victory comes only to those who hold on.

To the writer to the Hebrews, life was a journey that made its way to the presence of Christ. It was therefore never something that could be allowed to drift; it was its end which made the process of life all-important, and only those who endured to the end would be saved.

Here is a summons never to be less than our best, and always to remember that the end comes. If life is the road to Christ, no one can afford to miss it or to stop half-way.

THE CHRISTIAN HOPE

Hebrews 11:1–3

> Faith means that we are certain of the things we hope for, convinced of the things we do not see. It was because of faith that the men of old time had their record attested. It is by faith that we understand that the world was fashioned by the word of God, so that what is seen came into being out of what is unseen.

To the writer to the Hebrews, faith is a hope that is absolutely certain that what it believes is true and that what it expects will come. It is not the hope which looks forward with wistful longing; it is the hope which looks forward with utter conviction. In the early days of persecution, a humble Christian was brought before the judges. He told them that nothing they could do could shake him because he believed that, if he was true to God, God would be true to him. 'Do you really think', asked the judge, 'that the likes of you will go to God and his glory?' 'I do not think,' said the man, 'I know.' At one time, John Bunyan was tortured by uncertainty. 'Everyone doth think his own Religion rightest,' he said, 'both Jews and

Moors and Pagans; and how if all our Faith and Christ and Scriptures should be but a "Think so" too?' But, when the light broke, he ran out crying: 'Now I know! I know!' The Christian faith is a hope that has turned to certainty.

This Christian hope is such that it dictates every aspect of the way Christians conduct themselves. They live in it and they die in it; and it is the possession of it which makes them act as they do.

As the seventeenth-century Polish poet and hymn-writer Angelus Silesius sang:

> With Hope for pilgrim's staff I go,
>   And Patience is my travelling dress
> Wherewith through earthly weal and woe,
>   I fare to everlastingness.

James Moffatt distinguishes three directions in which the Christian hope operates.

(1) It is *belief in God against the world*. If we follow the world's standards, we may well have ease and comfort and prosperity; if we follow God's standards, we may well have pain and loss and unpopularity. It is the Christian conviction that it is better to suffer with God than to prosper with the world. In the book of Daniel, Shadrach, Meshach and Abednego are confronted with the choice of obeying Nebuchadnezzar and worshipping the king's image or obeying God and entering the fiery furnace. Without hesitation, they choose God (Daniel 3). When John Bunyan was to be put on trial, he said: 'With God's comfort in my poor soul, before I went down to the justices I begged of God that if I might do more good by being at liberty than in prison, then I might be set at liberty. But if not, his will be done.' The Christian attitude is that, in terms of eternity, it is better to stake everything on God than to trust to the rewards of the world.

(2) The Christian hope is *belief in the spirit against the senses*. The senses say to us: 'Take what you can touch and taste and handle and enjoy.' As the poet Robert Herrick wrote in 'Hesperides':

> Gather ye rosebuds while ye may,
>   Old Time is still a-flying;
> And this same flower that smiles today
>   Tomorrow will be dying.

The senses tell us to grasp the thing of the moment; the spirit tells us that there is something far beyond that. Christians believe in the spirit rather than the senses.

(3) The Christian hope is *belief in the future against the present*. Long ago, the Greek philosopher Epicurus said the chief purpose of life was pleasure. But he did not mean what so many people think he meant. He insisted that we must take the long view. The thing which is pleasant at the moment may sooner or later bring pain; the thing which at present hurts like fury may eventually bring joy. Christians are certain that in the long run no one can put aside the truth, for 'great is truth, and in the end she will prevail'.

It looked as if his judges had eliminated Socrates and as if Pilate had crushed Christ; but the verdict of the future reversed the verdict of the moment. The American Baptist preacher and author, Harry Emerson Fosdick, pointed out that Nero once condemned Paul, but the years have passed on and the time has come when people call their sons Paul and their dogs Nero.

It is easy to argue: 'Why should I refuse the pleasure of the moment for an uncertain future?' The Christian answer is that the future is *not* uncertain because it belongs to God; and it is enough that God has commanded and that God has promised.

The writer to the Hebrews goes on to say that it was precisely because the great heroes of the faith lived on that principle that they were approved by God. Every one of them refused what the world calls greatness and staked everything on God – and history proved them right.

The writer to the Hebrews goes further. He says that it is an act of faith to believe that God made this world, and adds that the things which are seen emerged from the things which are not seen. This was aiming a blow at the prevailing belief that God created the world out of existing matter which, being necessarily imperfect, meant that from the beginning this was an imperfect world. The writer to the Hebrews insists that God did not work with existing material but created the world from nothing. When he argued like this, he was not interested in the scientific side of the matter; he wanted to stress the fact that *this is God's world.*

If we can grasp the fact that this is God's world and that God is responsible for it, two things follow. First, we will use it as such. We will remember that everything in it is God's and will try to use it as God would have us use it. Second, we will remember that, even when it may not look like it, somehow God is in control. If we believe that this is God's world, then into our lives comes a new sense of responsibility and with it a new power of acceptance, for everything belongs to God and all is in his hands.

THE FAITH OF THE ACCEPTABLE OFFERING

Hebrews 11:4

It was by faith that Abel offered to God a fuller sacrifice than Cain and so gained the verdict of being a just man, for God himself witnessed to that fact on the grounds

of the gifts he brought; and, although he died because
of his faith, he is still speaking to us.

THE writer to the Hebrews begins his roll of honour of the
faithful with the name of Abel, whose story is in Genesis
4:1–15. Cain tilled the ground and brought to God an offering
of the fruits of the ground; Abel was a shepherd and brought
to God an offering from his flocks. God preferred the gift
of Abel to the gift of Cain, who, moved to bitter jealousy,
murdered his brother and became an outcast upon the earth.
In the original, the meaning of the story is difficult. There is
no indication why God preferred the gift of Abel to the gift
of Cain. It may well be that the only offering which anyone
can properly bring to God is that person's most precious
possession. This is *life itself*; and, to the Jews, blood always
stood for life. We can well understand that – because, when
the blood flows away, life ebbs away. On that principle, the
only true sacrifice to God was a sacrifice of blood. Abel's
sacrifice was of a living creature, Cain's was not; therefore
Abel's was the more acceptable.

But it may well be that the writer to the Hebrews is thinking
not only of the story as it is in Genesis but also of the legends
which gathered round it in Jewish folklore. The Jews themselves found the story puzzling and elaborated it in order to
find a reason for God's rejection of Cain and for Cain's murder
of Abel. The earliest legend tells how every time Eve had
children she gave birth to twins, a boy and a girl, and that
they were given to each other as man and wife. In the case of
Abel and Cain, Adam tried to change this and planned to
give the twin sister of Cain to Abel. Cain was bitterly dissatisfied. To settle the matter, Adam said to them: 'Go, my
sons, sacrifice to the Lord; and he whose sacrifice is accepted
shall have the young girl. Take each of you offerings in your

hand and go, sacrifice to the Lord and he will decide.' So Abel, who was a shepherd, took his best lamb to the place of sacrifice; but Cain, who was a tiller of the ground, took the poorest sheaf of corn he could find and laid it on the altar. Thereupon, fire descended from heaven and consumed Abel's offering so that not even the cinders were left, while Cain's was left untouched. Adam then gave the girl to Abel, and Cain was very angry. One day, Abel was asleep on a mountain; and Cain came upon him and took a stone and crushed his head. Then he threw the dead body on his back and carried it about because he did not know what to do with it. He saw two crows fighting and one killed the other, then dug a hole with its beak and buried it. Cain said: 'I have not the sense of this bird. I, too, will lay my brother in the ground,' and he did so.

The Jews had another story to explain the first murder. Cain and Abel could not agree as to what they should possess. So, Abel devised a scheme whereby they might bring an end to the disagreement. Cain took the earth and everything that did not move; Abel took everything that moved. But in Cain's heart there was still bitter envy. One day, he said to his brother: 'Remove your foot; you are standing on my property; the plain is mine.' Abel ran to the hills but Cain pursued him, saying: 'The hills are mine.' Abel took refuge on the mountains, but Cain still pursued him, saying: 'The mountains, too, are mine.' And so, in his envy, he hunted his brother until he killed him.

Behind this story lie two great truths. First, there is *envy*. Even the Greeks saw its horror. The great orator and statesman Demosthenes said: 'Envy is the sign of a nature that is altogether evil.' Euripides, the dramatist, said: 'Envy is the greatest of all diseases.' There was a Greek proverb which said: 'Envy has no place in the choir of God.' Envy leads to bitterness, bitterness to hatred, and hatred to murder. Envy is that poison which can poison all life and kill all goodness. Second, there is this strange and eerie thought that Cain had discovered a new sin. One of the old Greek fathers said: 'Up to this time, no one had died so that Cain should know how to kill. The devil instructed him in this in a dream.' It was Cain who introduced murder into the world. There is condemnation for the sinner; but there is still greater condemnation for the person who teaches another to sin. Anyone who does such a thing is banished from the face of God, just as Cain was.

So, the writer to the Hebrews says: 'Although he died for his faith, he is still speaking to us.' Moffatt comments: 'Death is never the last word in the life of a righteous man.' When people leave this world, they leave something in it. They may leave something which will grow and spread like a disease; or they may leave something fine which continues always to blossom and flourish. They leave an influence of good or ill; everyone who dies goes on speaking. May God grant that we leave behind not a germ of evil but a lovely thing in which the lives of those who come afterwards will find blessing.

WALKING WITH GOD

Hebrews 11:5–6

> It was by faith that Enoch was transferred from this to the other life so that he did not die but passed from men's sight, because God took him from one life to the other. For, before this change came to him, it was testified that he pleased God. Apart from faith it is impossible to please God, for he who approaches God must believe that God is, and that he is the rewarder of those who spend their lives seeking him.

IN the Old Testament, the life of Enoch is summed up in one sentence: 'Enoch walked with God; then he was no more, because God took him' (Genesis 5:24). Many legends gathered around his name. He was said to be the first man skilled in tailoring and in sewing and that he taught others how to cut out skins in the proper shape to make garments. He was said to be the first to teach people to make shoes to protect their feet. He was said to be the first to write things down and to teach from books.

Legend tells that the Angel of Death made a pact of friendship with Enoch. Enoch made three requests of him. First, to die and come back again so that he might know what death was like. Second, to see the place where the wicked went so that he might know what the punishment of evil men and women was like. Both these requests were granted. His third request was to be allowed to see into Paradise so that he might see what the blessed who entered there enjoyed. This also was granted; but Enoch, having been granted a glimpse of Paradise, never came back to earth again.

The simple statement in Genesis has a kind of mystical quality. In itself, it does not say how Enoch died. It simply says that in God's good time he passed serenely from this earth. There are two especially famous interpretations of the death of Enoch.

(1) The Book of Wisdom (4:10ff.) has the idea that God took Enoch to himself when he was still young to save him from the infection of this world. He was taken away while he lived among sinners. He was snatched away in case evil should change his understanding or guile deceive his soul. This is another way of putting the famous classical saying: 'Those whom the gods love die young.' It looks on death as a reward. It means that God loved Enoch so much that he

removed him before age and degeneration descended hand in hand upon him.

(2) Philo, the great Alexandrian Jewish interpreter, saw in Enoch the great model of *repentance*. He was changed by repentance from the life that is apart from God to the life that walks with God.

The writer to the Hebrews reads into the simple statement of the Old Testament passage the idea that Enoch did not die at all but that in some mystic way God took him to himself. But surely the meaning is much simpler. In a wicked and corrupt generation, Enoch walked with God; and so, when the end came to him, there was no shock or interruption. Death merely took him into God's nearer presence. Because he walked with God when others were walking away from him, day by day Enoch came nearer to God, and death was no more than the last step that took him into the very presence of that God with whom he had always walked.

We cannot think of Enoch without thinking of the different attitudes to death. The sheer serenity of the Old Testament statement, so simple and yet so moving, points forward to the Christian attitude.

(1) There are those who have thought of death as *mysterious and inexplicable*. The nineteenth-century writer and artist William Morris wrote:

> Death have we hated, knowing not what it meant.

Francis Bacon, the philosopher, said: 'Men fear death as children fear to go in the dark.' To some, it has always been the terrifying unknown, giving rise to what Hamlet called 'that dread of something after death'.

(2) There are those who simply have seen in death *the one inevitable thing in life*. Shakespeare makes Caesar say in *Julius Caesar*:

It seems to me most strange that men should fear;
Seeing that death, a necessary end,
Will come when it will come.

And, in *Cymbeline*, he writes with a strange fatalistic beauty:

Fear no more the heat o' the sun,
    Nor the furious winter's rages;
Thou thy worldly task hast done,
    Home art gone and ta'en thy wages:
Golden lads and girls all must,
As chimney-sweepers, come to dust.

Fear no more the frown o' the great,
    Thou art past the tyrant's stroke:
Care no more to clothe and eat;
    To thee the reed is as the oak:
The sceptre, learning, physic must
All follow this, and come to dust.

Fear no more the lightning-flash,
    Nor the all-dreaded thunder-stone;
Fear not slander, censure rash;
    Thou hast finish'd joy and moan:
All lovers young, all lovers must
Consign to thee, and come to dust.

Death is inevitable, and there is nothing to be gained by struggling against it.

(3) Some have seen in death *sheer extinction*. It was that loveliest of Roman poets, Catullus, who pleaded with Lesbia for her kisses because the night was coming:

Lesbia mine, let's live and love!
Give no doit for tattle of
Crabbed old censorious men;
Suns may set and rise again,
But when our short day takes flight
Sleep we must one endless night.

To die was to go out to nothingness and be lost in an eternal sleep.

(4) Some have seen in death *the supreme terror and the unmitigated evil*. In *Measure for Measure*, Shakespeare makes Claudio say:

> Death is a fearful thing.
> Ay, but to die, and go we know not where;
> To lie in cold obstruction, and to rot;
> This sensible warm motion to become
> A kneaded clod; and the delighted spirit
> To bathe in fiery floods, or to reside
> In thrilling region of thick-ribbed ice;
> To be imprison'd in the viewless winds,
> And blown with restless violence round about
> The pendent world . . .
> The weariest and most loathed worldly life
> That age, ache, penury and imprisonment
> Can lay on nature, is a paradise
> To what we fear of death.

To Claudio, the worst and bitterest experiences of life were to be preferred to death. W. S. Gilbert wrote in *The Yeomen of the Guard*:

> Is life a boon?
> 　If so, it must befall
> 　That Death, whene'er he call,
> Must call too soon.

Robert Burns wrote of the early death of Highland Mary:

> But oh! fell death's untimely frost
> 　That nipt my flower sae early!

There are those who have seen only the grim terrorizer and despoiler in death.

(5) Many have seen in death *release*. Weary of the world and of life, they have seen it as escape. In 'The Eve of Saint Agnes', Keats said that he had been 'half in love with easeful death'. Shakespeare in one of his sonnets cried:

> Tir'd with all these, for restful death I cry.

The seventeenth-century poet and dramatist Nicholas Rowe wrote: 'Death is the privilege of human nature.' The Stoics held that the gods had given people the gift of life and the still greater gift of taking their own lives away. Swinburne, best of all, caught this mood of world-weariness in 'The Garden of Proserpine':

> From too much love of living,
>   From hope and fear set free,
> We thank with brief thanksgiving
>   Whatever gods may be
> That no life lives forever,
> That dead men rise up never;
> That even the weariest river
>   Winds somewhere safe to sea.
>
> Then star nor sun shall waken,
>   Nor any change of light;
> Nor sound of waters shaken,
>   Nor any sound or sight;
> Nor wintry leaves nor vernal
> Nor days nor things diurnal;
> Only the sleep eternal
>   In an eternal night.

There are those for whom death is good because it is the end of life.

(6) Some have seen in death *transition* – not an end, but a stage on the way; not a door closing, but a door opening. In 'Resignation', Longfellow wrote:

> There is no Death! What seems so is transition;
> 　This life of mortal breath
> Is but a suburb of the life elysian,
> 　Whose portal we call death.

The nineteenth-century novelist and poet George Meredith
wrote:

> Death met I too,
> And saw the dawn glow through.

To these and others like them, death has always been a call to
come up higher, a crossing from the dark to the dawn.

(7) Some have seen death as an *adventure*. As J. M. Barrie
made Peter Pan say: 'To die will be an awfully big adventure.'
Charles Frohman, who had known Barrie so well, went down
when the *Lusitania* sank in the disaster of 7 May 1915. His
last words were: 'Why fear death? It is the most beautiful
adventure in life.' An old scholar who was dying turned to
his friends: 'Do you realize', he said, 'that in an hour or two
I will know the answers for which we have been searching
all our lives?' To these, death is the adventure of supreme
discovery.

(8) Above all, there are those, like Enoch, who have seen
death as an *entering into the nearer presence* of the one with
whom they have lived for so long. If we have lived with
Christ, we may die in the certainty that we go to be forever
with our Lord.

In this passage, the writer to the Hebrews lays down, in
addition, the two great foundation acts of faith of the Christian
life.

(1) *We must believe in God*. There can be no such thing as
religion without that belief. Religion began when men and
women became aware of God; it ceases when they live a life
in which for them God does not exist.

(2) *We must believe that God is interested.* As the writer to the Hebrews put it, we must believe that God is the rewarder of those who diligently seek him.

There were those in the ancient world who believed in the gods, but they believed that they lived out in the spaces between the worlds, entirely unaware of human life. 'God', said the philosopher Epicurus as a first principle, 'does nothing.' There are many who believe in God but do not believe that he cares.

It has been said that no astronomer can be an atheist; but it has also been said that an astronomer is bound to believe that God is a mathematician. But a God who is a mathematician need not care. God has been called the First Principle, the First Cause, the Creative Energy, the Life Force. These are the statements of people who believe in God, but not in a God who cares.

When the Roman emperor Marcus Aurelius was asked why he believed in the gods, he said: 'True, the gods are not discernible by human sight, but neither have I seen my soul and yet I honour it. So, I believe in the gods and I honour them, because again and again I have experienced their power.' It was not logic but life that convinced him of the gods.

The Stoic philosophers believed in the power of the gods over the universe. Seneca said: 'The first essential of the worship of the gods is to believe that there are gods . . . and to know those gods who preside over the world, because they control the universe with their power, and work for the safety of the whole human race, while they still remember each individual person.' Epictetus said: 'You must know that the most important thing in reverence for the gods is to have right beliefs that they are and that they order all things righteously and well.'

We must believe not only that God exists but also that he cares and is involved in the human situation. For Christians that is easy, for God came to the world in Jesus Christ to tell us how much he cares.

THE MAN WHO BELIEVED IN GOD'S MESSAGE

Hebrews 11:7

> It was by faith that Noah, when he had been informed by God about things that were still unseen, reverently accepted the message and built an ark to preserve his household in safety. Through that faith he passed judgment on the world and became an heir of the righteousness which is the result of faith.

THE Old Testament story of Noah is in Genesis 6–8. The earth was so wicked that God decided that there was no alternative but to destroy it. He told Noah his decision and instructed him to build an ark in which he and his family and the representatives of the animal world might be saved. With reverence and obedience, Noah took God at his word, and so in the destruction of the world he was preserved.

As is usually the case, legend has added numerous details to this story. The writer to the Hebrews must have known these legends, and they must have helped to add vividness to the picture in his mind. One story tells how Noah was in doubt as to the shape he was to give the ark. God revealed to him that it was to be modelled on a bird's belly and was to be constructed of teak wood. Noah planted a teak tree, and in twenty years it grew to such a size that out of it he was able to build the entire ark. Another story tells that, after he had been forewarned by God, Noah made a bell of plane wood, about five feet high, and that he sounded it every day – morning, noon and evening. When he was asked why, he answered: 'To warn you that God will send a deluge to destroy you all.' Another story tells that, when Noah was building the ark, the people laughed at him and thought that he was mad. But he said to them: 'Though you mock me now, the time will come when I shall do the same to you; for you will learn to your cost who it is that punishes the wicked in this world and reserves for them a further punishment in the world to come.'

Even more than Abel and Enoch, Noah stands out as a man of faith.

(1) *Noah took God at his word.* He believed the message which God sent him. God's message might have appeared to be foolishness at the time; but Noah believed it and staked everything on it. Obviously, if he was going to accept that word of God, he had to lay aside his normal activities and concentrate on doing what that message commanded. Noah's life was one continued and concentrated preparation for what God had said would come.

The choice comes to each one of us either to listen to or to disregard the message of God. We may live as if that message is of no importance or as if it is the most important thing in the world. To put it another way: Noah was the man who heeded the warning of God; and, because he heeded, he was saved from disaster. God's warning comes to us in many ways. It may come from conscience; it may come from some direct word of God to our souls; it may come from the advice or the rebuke of some good and godly person; it may leap out at us from the pages of the Bible or challenge us in some sermon. Wherever it comes from, we neglect it at our peril.

(2) *Noah was not deterred by the mockery of others.* When the sun was shining, his conduct must have looked like that of a fool. Who in their right mind would build a great hulk of a ship on dry land far from the sea? Those who take God's

word may often have to adopt a course of action which looks like madness.

We have only to think of the early days of the Church. One man meets a friend. He says to him: 'I have decided to become a Christian.' The other man replies: 'Do you know what happens to Christians? They are outlaws. They are imprisoned, thrown to the lions, crucified, burned.' The first man replies: 'I know.' And the other says: 'You must be mad.'

It is one of the hardest challenges of Christianity that we have to be prepared sometimes to be a fool for Jesus' sake. We should never forget that there was a day when Jesus' friends came and tried to get him to go home because they thought that he was mad. The wisdom of God is so often foolishness to the world.

(3) *Noah's faith was a judgment on others*. That is why, at least in one sense, it is dangerous to be a Christian. It is not that Christians are self-righteous; it is not that they are censorious; it is not that they go about finding fault with other people; it is not that they say: 'I told you so.' It often happens that, simply by being themselves, Christians pass judgment on other people. Alcibiades, that brilliant but wild young man of Athens, used to say to Socrates: 'Socrates, I hate you, for every time I meet you, you show me what I am.' One of the finest men who ever lived in Athens was Aristides, who was called 'the just'. But they voted to banish him. One man, asked why he had voted in that way, answered: 'Because I am tired of hearing Aristides called "the just".' There is danger in goodness, for in its light evil stands condemned.

(4) *Noah was righteous through faith*. It so happens that he is the first man in the Bible to be called *dikaios*, *righteous* (Genesis 6:9). His goodness consisted in the fact that he took God at his word. When others broke God's commandments, Noah kept them; when others were deaf to God's warnings,

Noah listened to them; when others laughed at God, Noah held him in reverence. It has been said of Noah that 'he threw the dark scepticism of the world into relief against his own shining faith in God'. In an age when people disregarded God, for Noah he was the supreme reality in the world.

THE ADVENTURE AND THE PATIENCE OF FAITH

Hebrews 11:8-10

> It was by faith that Abraham, when he was called, showed his obedience by going out to a place which he was going to receive as an inheritance, and he went out not knowing where he was to go. It was by faith that he sojourned in the land that had been promised to him, as though it had been a foreign land, living in tents, in the same way as did Isaac and Jacob, who were his co-heirs in the promise of it. For he was waiting for the city which has foundations, whose architect and builder is God.

THE call of Abraham is told with dramatic simplicity in Genesis 12:1. Jewish and middle-eastern legends gathered largely round Abraham's name, and some of them must have been known to the writer to the Hebrews. The legends tell how Abraham was the son of Terah, commander of the armies of Nimrod. When Abraham was born, a very vivid star appeared in the sky and seemed to obliterate the others. Nimrod sought to murder the infant, but Abraham was concealed in a cave and his life was saved. It was in that cave that the first vision of God came to him. When he was a youth, he came out of the cave and stood looking across the face of the desert. The sun rose in all its glory, and Abraham said: 'Surely the sun is God, the Creator!' So he knelt down and worshipped the sun. But when evening came, the sun sank in the west and Abraham said: 'No! the author of creation cannot set!' The moon arose in the east and the stars came out. Then Abraham said: 'The moon must be God and the stars his host!' So he knelt down and adored the moon. But after the night had passed, the moon sank and the sun rose again and Abraham said: 'Truly these heavenly bodies are no gods, for they obey law; I will worship the one who imposed the law upon them.'

The Arabs have a different legend. They tell how Abraham saw many flocks and herds and said to his mother: 'Who is the lord of these?' She answered: 'Your father, Terah.' 'And who is the lord of Terah?' the young Abraham asked. 'Nimrod,' said his mother. 'And who is the lord of Nimrod?' asked Abraham. His mother told him to be quiet and not push questions too far; but already Abraham's thoughts were reaching out to the one who is the God of all. The legends go on to tell that Terah not only worshipped twelve idols, one for each of the months, but was also a manufacturer of idols. One day, Abraham was left in charge of the shop. People came in to buy idols. Abraham would ask them how old they were and they would answer perhaps 50 or 60 years of age. 'Woe to a man of such an age', said Abraham, 'who adores the work of one day!' A strong and fit man of 70 came in. Abraham asked him his age and then said: 'You fool to adore a god who is younger than yourself!' A woman came in with a dish of meat for the gods. Abraham took a stick and smashed all the idols but one, in whose hands he set the stick he had used. Terah returned and was angry. Abraham said: 'My father, a woman brought this dish of meat for your gods; they all wanted to have it and the strongest knocked the heads off the rest, in case they should eat it all.' Terah said: 'That is impossible, for they are made of wood and stone.' And

Abraham answered: 'Let your own ear hear what your own mouth has spoken!'

All these legends give us a vivid picture of Abraham searching after God and being dissatisfied with the idolatry of his people. So, when God's call came to him, he was ready to go out into the unknown to find him. Abraham is the supreme example of faith.

(1) Abraham's faith was *the faith that was ready for adventure*. God's summons meant that he had to leave home and family and business; yet he went. He had to go out into the unknown; yet he went. In the best of us, there is a certain timidity. We wonder just what will happen to us if we take God at his word and act on his commands and promises.

Bishop Lesslie Newbigin tells of the negotiations which led to the formation of the United Church of South India. He took part in these negotiations and in the long discussions which were necessary. Things were frequently held up by cautious people who wanted to know just where each step was taking them, until in the end the chairman reminded them that Christians have no right to ask where they are going.

Most of us live a cautious life on the principle of safety first; but, to live the Christian life, it is necessary to have a certain reckless willingness to be adventurous. If faith can see every step of the way, it is not really faith. It is sometimes necessary for Christians to take the way to which the voice of God is calling them without knowing what the consequences will be. Like Abraham, they have to go out not knowing where they are going.

(2) Abraham's faith was *the faith which had patience*. When he reached the promised land, he was never allowed to possess it. He had to wander in it, a stranger and a tent-dweller, as the people of Israel were some day to wander in

the wilderness. For Abraham, God's promise was never fully fulfilled; and yet he never abandoned his faith.

It is a characteristic of the best of us that we are in a hurry. To wait is even harder than to be adventurous. The hardest time of all is the time in between. At the moment of decision, there is the excitement and the thrill; at the moment of achievement, there is the glow and glory of satisfaction; but, in the intervening time, it is necessary to have the ability to wait and work and watch when nothing seems to be happening. It is then that we are most liable to give up our hopes and lower our ideals and sink into an apathy whose dreams are dead. Men and women of faith are people whose hope is flaming brightly and whose effort is intensely strenuous even in the grey days when there is nothing to do but to wait.

(3) Abraham's faith was *the faith which was looking beyond this world*. The later legends believed that, at the moment of his call, Abraham was given a glimpse of the new Jerusalem. In the Apocalypse of Baruch, God says: 'I showed it to my servant Abraham by night' (4:4). In 2 Esdras [4 Ezra], the writer says: 'And when they were committing iniquity in your sight, you chose for yourself one of them, whose name was Abraham; you loved him, and to him alone you revealed the end of times, secretly by night' (3:13–14). No one ever did anything great without a vision which made it possible to face the difficulties and discouragements of the way. To Abraham there was given the vision; and, even when his body was wandering in Palestine, his soul was at home with God. God cannot give us the vision unless we allow him to; but, if we are patient and look to him, even in earth's desert places he will send us the vision, and with it the toil and trouble of the way all become worth while.

BELIEVING THE INCREDIBLE

Hebrews 11:11–12

> It was by faith that Sarah, too, received power to conceive and to bear a son, although she was beyond the age for it, for she believed that he who gave the promise could be absolutely relied upon. So from one man, and he a man whose body had lost its vitality, there were born descendants, as many as the stars of the sky in multitude, as countless as the sand upon the seashore.

THE story of the promise of a son to Abraham and Sarah is told in Genesis 17:15–22, 18:9–15 and 21:1–8. Its wonder is that Abraham and Sarah were each 90 years old, long past the age of having children; and yet, according to the old story, that promise was made and came true.

The reaction of Abraham and Sarah to the promise of God followed a threefold course.

(1) It began with sheer *incredulity*. When Abraham heard the promise, he fell upon his face and laughed (Genesis 17:17). When Sarah heard it, she laughed to herself (Genesis 18:12). On first hearing of the promises of God, the human reaction is often that this is far too good to be true. In words from F. W. Faber's hymn:

> How thou canst think so well of us,
> And be the God thou art,
> Is darkness to my intellect,
> But sunshine to my heart.

There is no mystery in all creation like the love of God. That he should love us and suffer and die for us is something that staggers us into sheer incredulity. That is why the Christian message is the *gospel*, *good news*; it is news so good that it is almost impossible to believe it to be true.

(2) It passed into *dawning realization*. After the incredulity came the dawning realization that *this was God who was speaking*; and God cannot lie. The Jews used to lay it down as a primary law for a teacher that he must never promise his pupils what he was unwilling or unable to perform; to do so would be to introduce pupils at an early stage to broken promises. When we remember that the one who makes the promise is *God*, we begin to realize that, however astonishing that promise may be, it must nonetheless be true.

(3) It culminated in *the ability to believe in the impossible*. That Abraham and Sarah should have a child, humanly speaking, was impossible. As Sarah said: 'Who would ever have said to Abraham that Sarah would nurse children?' (Genesis 21:7). But, by the grace and the power of God, the impossible became true. There is something here to challenge and uplift every heart. The Italian statesman Count Cavour said that the first essential of a statesman is 'the sense of the possible'.

When we listen to people planning and arguing and thinking aloud, we get the impression of a vast number of things in this world which are known to be desirable but which are dismissed as impossible. People spend the greater part of their lives putting limitations on the power of God. Faith is the ability to take hold of that grace which is sufficient for all things in such a way that the things which are humanly impossible become divinely possible. With God, all things are possible; and, therefore, the word *impossible* has no place in the vocabulary of the individual Christian or of the Christian Church.

STRANGERS AND NOMADS

Hebrews 11:13–16

> All these died without obtaining possession of the promises. They only saw them from far away and greeted them from afar, and they admitted that they were strangers and sojourners upon the earth. Now, people who speak like that make it quite clear that they are searching for a fatherland. If they were thinking of the land from which they had come out, they would have had time to return. In point of fact, they were reaching out after something better, I mean, the heavenly country. It was because of that that God was not ashamed to be called their God, for he had prepared a city for them.

NONE of the patriarchs entered into the full possession of the promises that God had made to Abraham. To the end of their days they were nomads, never living a settled life in a settled land. They had to be constantly moving on. Certain great permanent truths emerge from them.

(1) They lived as permanent strangers. The writer to the Hebrews uses three vivid Greek words about them.

(a) In 11:13, he calls them *xenoi*. *Xenos* is the word for *a stranger and a foreigner*. In the ancient world, the fate of strangers was hard. They were regarded with hatred and suspicion and contempt. In Sparta, *xenos* was the equivalent of *barbaros*, barbarian. One man writes complaining that he was despised 'because I am a *xenos*'. Another writes that, however poor a home is, it is better to live at home than *epi xenēs*, in a foreign country. When clubs had their common meal, those who sat down to it were divided into *members* and *xenoi*. *Xenos* can even mean a *refugee*. All their lives, the patriarchs were foreigners in a land that was never their own.

(b) In 11:9, he uses the word *paroikein, to stay for a time*, of Abraham. A *paroikos* was *a resident alien*. The word is used of the Jews when they were captives in Babylon and in Egypt. Anyone called *paroikos* was not considered much above a slave in the social scale and had to pay an alien tax. Such people were always outsiders and only became members of the community as a result of payment.

(c) In 11:13, he uses the word *parepidēmos*. A *parepidēmos* was a person who was staying there temporarily and who had a permanent home somewhere else. Sometimes, the stay was strictly limited. A *parepidēmos* was someone in lodgings, someone without a home in a particular place at a particular time. All their lives, the patriarchs were men who had no settled place that they could call home. It is to be noted that, in the ancient world, to dwell in a foreign land was considered humiliating; a certain stigma was attached to the foreigner in any country. In the *Letter of Aristeas*, the writer says: 'It is a fine thing to live and to die in one's native land; a foreign land brings contempt to poor men and shame to rich men, for there is the lurking suspicion that they have been exiled for the evil they have done.' In Ecclesiasticus (29:22–8), there is a wistful passage:

> Better is the life of the poor under their own crude roof
>   than sumptuous food in the house of others.
> Be content with little or much,
>   and you will hear no reproach for being a guest.
>
> It is a miserable life to go from house to house;
>   as a guest you should not open your mouth;
> you will play the host and provide drink without being
>   thanked
>   and besides this you will hear rude words like these:
> 'Come here, stranger, prepare the table;
>   let me eat what you have there.'

'Be off, stranger, for an honoured guest is here;
   my brother has come for a visit, and I need the guest-
      room.'
It is hard for a sensible person to bear
   scolding about lodging and the insults of the
      moneylender.

At any time, it is an unhappy thing to be a stranger in a foreign
land; but, in the ancient world, to this natural unhappiness
there was added the bitterness of humiliation.

All their days, the patriarchs were strangers in a strange
land. That image became a picture of the Christian life and is
found in the works of the early Church fathers. Tertullian
said of the Christian: 'He knows that on earth he has a
pilgrimage but that his dignity is in heaven.' Clement of
Alexandria said: 'We have no fatherland on earth.' Augustine
said: 'We are sojourners exiled from our fatherland.' It was
not that the Christians were foolishly other-worldly, detaching
themselves from the life and work of this world; but they
always remembered that they were people on the way. There
is an unwritten saying of Jesus: 'The world is a bridge. The
wise will pass over it but will not build a house upon it.'
Christians regard themselves as the pilgrims of eternity.

(2) In spite of everything, these men never lost their vision
and their hope. However long that hope might be in coming
true, its light always shone in their eyes. However long the
way might be, they never stopped tramping along it. Robert
Louis Stevenson said: 'It is better to travel hopefully than to
arrive.' They never wearily gave up the journey; they lived in
hope and died in expectation.

(3) In spite of everything, they never wanted to go back.
Their descendants, when they were in the desert, often
expressed a wish to go back to the fleshpots of Egypt. But
not the patriarchs. They had begun, and it never struck them

to turn back. In flying, there is what is called *the point of no return*. When the aircraft has reached that point, *it cannot go back*. Its fuel supply has reached such a level that there is no option but to go on. One of the tragedies of life is the number of people who turn back just a little too soon. One further effort, a little more waiting, a little more hoping, would make the dream come true. Immediately a Christian has set out on some enterprise sent by God, he or she should feel that the point of no return has already been passed.

(4) These men were able to go on because they were haunted by the things beyond. People with the urge to travel are lured on by the thought of the countries they have not yet seen. Great artists or composers are driven by the thought of the performance they have not yet given and the wonder they have not yet produced. Robert Louis Stevenson tells of an old farmworker who spent all his days amid the muck of the cowshed. Someone asked him if he never got tired of it all. He answered: 'He that has something ayont [beyond] need never weary.' These men had the something beyond – and so may we.

(5) Because these men were what they were, God was not ashamed to be called their God. Above all things, he is the God of the brave adventurer. He loves the person who is ready to venture for his name. The prudent, comfort-loving individual is the very opposite of God. The one who goes out into the unknown and keeps going on will in the end arrive at God.

THE SUPREME SACRIFICE

Hebrews 11:17–19

> It was by faith that Abraham offered up Isaac when he was put to the test. He was willing to offer up even his

only son, although it had been said to him: 'It is in Isaac that your descendants will be named.' He was willing to do this, for he reckoned that God was able to raise him even from the dead. Hence he did receive him back, which is a parable of the resurrection.

THE Isaac story, told in Genesis 22:1–18, is that most dramatic account of how Abraham met the supreme test of the demand for the life of his own son. To some extent, this story has fallen into disrepute. Some people argue that it presents an unacceptable view of God. Or it is held that the point of the story is that it was in this way that Abraham learned that God did not desire human sacrifice. No doubt that is true; but, if we want to see this story at its greatest and as the writer to the Hebrews saw it, we must take it at its face value. It shows the response of a man who was asked to offer his own son to God.

(1) This story teaches us that we must be ready to sacrifice what is dearest to us for the sake of loyalty to God. There have been many who have sacrificed their careers to what they took to be the will of God. J. P. Struthers was the minister of the Reformed Presbyterian Church in Greenock, a little congregation which, it is neither false nor unkind to say, had a great past but no future. Had he been willing to forsake this church, any pulpit in the land was open to him and the most dazzling ecclesiastical rewards were his; but he sacrificed them all for the sake of what he considered to be loyalty to God's will.

Sometimes, people may have to sacrifice personal relationships. They may feel called by God to a task in a sphere which is difficult and in a place that is unattractive, and it may be that the person they hoped to marry will not face it with them. They must choose between the will of God and the relationship which means so much to them. When John

Bunyan was in prison, he was thinking of what would happen to his family if he was executed. In particular, the thought of his little blind daughter, who was so dear to him, haunted him: 'O,' he said, 'I saw in this condition I was a man who was pulling down his house upon the head of his wife and children; yet, thought I, I must do it, I must do it.' In words from William Cowper's hymn 'O for a closer walk with God':

> The dearest idol I have known,
>   Whate'er that idol be,
> Help me to tear it from thy throne,
>   And worship only thee.

Abraham was the man who would sacrifice even the dearest thing in life for God. Time after time in the early Church, it happened. In a home, one partner became a Christian and the other did not; the children became Christians and the parents did not. The sword came down upon that home; and, unless there had been men and women who counted Christ dearer than all else, there would be no Christianity today.

God must come first in our lives, or he comes nowhere. There is a story of two children who had been given a toy Noah's Ark as a present. They had been listening to the Old Testament stories, and decided that they too would offer a sacrifice. They examined the animals in their toy ark and finally decided on *a sheep with a broken leg*. The only thing they would offer was a broken toy they could well do without. That is the way in which so many people would like to sacrifice to God; but only the dearest and the best is good enough for him.

(2) Abraham is the model of the individual who accepts what is beyond understanding. To him there had come this incomprehensible demand. It did not make sense. The promise was that in Isaac his seed would grow and grow until he

became a mighty nation in which all others would be blessed. On the life of Isaac depended the promise; and now God seemed to want to take that life away. As the fourth-century churchman John Chrysostom put it: 'The things of God seemed to fight against the things of God, and faith fought with faith, and the commandment fought with the promise.' For everyone at some time, there comes something for which there seems to be no reason and which defies explanation. It is then that we are faced with life's hardest battle – to accept when we cannot understand. At such a time, there is only one thing to do – to obey and to do so without resentment, saying: 'God, you are love! I build my faith on that.'

(3) Abraham is the model of the individual who, with the test, found a way of escape. If we take God at his word and stake everything on him, even when there seems to be nothing but a blank wall in front of us, the way of escape will open up.

THE FAITH WHICH DEFEATS DEATH

Hebrews 11:20-2

> It was by faith that Isaac blessed Jacob and Esau in the things concerning the future. It was by faith that Jacob, when he was dying, blessed each of the sons of Joseph and prayed leaning on the head of his staff. It was by faith that Joseph, as he came to the end, had in his mind the days when the children of Israel would leave Egypt, and gave instructions concerning his bones.

ONE thing links these three examples of faith together. In each case, it was the faith of someone to whom death was very near. The blessing which Isaac gave is in Genesis 27:28–9, 39–40. Given after Isaac had said: 'See, I am old; I do not know the day of my death' (Genesis 27:2), it was: 'May God give you of the dew of heaven, and of the fatness of the earth, and plenty of grain and wine. Let peoples serve you, and nations bow down to you.' The blessing of Jacob is given in Genesis 48:9–22. The story has just said that 'the time of Israel's death drew near' (Genesis 47:29). The blessing was: 'In them let my name be perpetuated, and the name of my ancestors Abraham and Isaac; and let them grow into a multitude on the earth' (Genesis 48:16). The incident from the life of Joseph comes from Genesis 50:22–6. When Joseph was near to death, he made the Israelites take an oath that they would not leave his bones in Egypt but would take them with them when they went out to possess the promised land, which in due course they did (Exodus 13:19; Joshua 24:32).

The point which the writer to the Hebrews wishes to make is that all three men died without having entered into the promise that God had made, the promise of the promised land and of greatness to the nation of Israel. Isaac was still a nomad, Jacob was an exile in Egypt, Joseph had attained to greatness but it was the greatness of a stranger in a strange land; and yet they never doubted that the promise would come true. They died not in despair but in hope. Their faith defeated death.

There is something of permanent greatness here. The thought in the minds of all these men was the same: 'God's promise is true, for he never breaks a promise. I may not live to see it, death may come to me before that promise becomes a fact; but I am a link in its fulfilment. Whether or not that promise comes depends on me.' Here is the great function of life. Our hopes may never become reality, but we must live in such a way that we shall hasten their coming. It may not be given to everyone to enter into the fullness of the promises of God, but it is given to every one of us to live with such faithfulness as to bring nearer the day when others will enter into it. To all of us is given the tremendous task of helping God make his promises come true.

FAITH AND ITS SECRET

Hebrews 11:23–9

It was by faith that Moses, when he was born, was kept hidden for three months by his parents, because they saw that the child was beautiful – and they did not fear the edict of the king. It was by faith that Moses, when he grew to manhood, refused to be called the son of Pharaoh's daughter and chose rather to suffer evil with the people of God than to enjoy the transient pleasures of sin, for he considered that a life of reproach for the sake of the Messiah was greater wealth than the treasures of Egypt, for he kept his eyes fixed upon his reward. It was by faith that he left Egypt, unmoved by the blazing anger of the king, for he could face all things as one who sees him who is invisible. It was by faith that he carried out the Passover and the sprinkling of blood, so that the destroying angel might not touch the children of his people. It was by faith that they crossed the Red Sea as if they were going through dry land and that the Egyptians, when they ventured to try to do so, were engulfed.

To the Jews, Moses was the supreme figure in their history. He was the leader who had rescued them from slavery and who had received the law of their lives from God. To the writer of the letter to the Hebrews, Moses was pre-eminently the man of faith. In this story, as James Moffatt points out, there are five different acts of faith. As with the other great characters whose names are included in this roll of honour of

God's faithful ones, many legends and elaborations had gathered round the name of Moses, and doubtless the writer of this letter had them also in mind.

(1) There was the faith of Moses' parents. The story of their action is told in Exodus 2:1–10. Exodus 1:15–22 tells how the king of Egypt, in his hatred, tried to wipe out the male children of the Israelites by having them killed at birth. Legend tells how Amram and Jochebed, the parents of Moses (Exodus 6:20), were worried by the decree of Pharaoh. As a result, Amram had no contact with his wife, not because he did not love her, but because he wanted to spare her the sorrow of seeing her children killed. For three years they were apart, and then Miriam prophesied: 'My parents shall have another son, who shall deliver Israel out of the hands of the Egyptians.' She said to her father: 'What have you done? You have sent your wife away out of your house, because you could not trust the Lord God that he would protect the child that might be born to you.' So Amram, shamed into trusting God, took back his wife; and in due course Moses was born. He was so lovely a child that his parents determined to hide him in their house. This they did for three months. Then, according to the legend, the Egyptians struck upon a cruel scheme. The king was determined that hidden children should be sought out and killed. Now, when a child hears another child cry, the first child will cry too. So, Egyptian mothers were sent into the homes of the Israelites with their babies; there they pricked their babies until they cried. This made the hidden children of the Israelites cry, too, and so they were discovered and killed. In view of this, Amram and Jochebed decided to make a little ark and to entrust their child to it on the waters of the Nile.

That Moses was born at all was an act of faith; that he was preserved was another. He began by being the child of faith.

(2) The second act of faith was Moses' loyalty to his own people. The story is told in Exodus 2:11–14. Again, the legends help to light up the picture. When Moses was entrusted to the waters of the Nile, he was found by the daughter of Pharaoh, whose name is given as Bithia, or more commonly Thermouthis. She was entranced by his beauty. Legend says that when she drew the ark out of the water, the archangel Gabriel boxed the ears of the little baby to make him cry so that the heart of Thermouthis might be touched as she saw the little face puckered in sorrow and the eyes full of tears. Thermouthis, much to her sorrow, was childless; so she took the baby Moses home, and cared for him as her own son. He grew to be so beautiful that people turned in the street, and even stopped their work, to look at him. He was so wise that he was far ahead of all other children in learning and in knowledge. When he was still a child, Thermouthis took him to Pharaoh and told him how she had found him. She placed him in his arms, and he was so taken with the child that he embraced him and, at the request of Thermouthis, he promised to make him his heir. As a joke, he took his crown and placed it on the child's head; but the infant snatched the crown from his head and flung it on the ground and trampled on it. Pharaoh's wise men were full of foreboding that this child would some day trample the royal power under foot. They wanted to destroy Moses there and then. But a test was proposed: they set before the child a bowl of precious stones and a bowl of live coals. If he put out his hand and touched the jewels, that would prove that he was so wise that he was a danger; if he put out his hands and touched the coals, that would prove that he was so stupid that he was no danger. The infant Moses was about to touch the jewels when Gabriel took his hand and put it on the coals. His finger was burnt; he put the burnt finger in his mouth and burnt his

mouth; that, they say, was why he was not a good speaker (Exodus 4:10) but stammered all his life.

So, Moses was spared. He was brought up in great luxury. He was heir to the kingdom. He became one of the greatest of all Egyptian generals; in particular, he conquered the Ethiopians when they were threatening Egypt, and in the end was married to an Ethiopian princess. But, all the time, he had never forgotten his fellow Israelites; and the day came when he decided to ally himself with the downtrodden children of Israel and say goodbye to the future of riches and royalty that he might have had.

Moses gave up earthly glory for the sake of the people of God. Christ gave up his glory for the sake of all humanity, and accepted scourging and shame and a terrible death. Moses in his day and generation shared in the sufferings of Christ, choosing the loyalty that led to suffering rather than the comfort which led to earthly glory. He knew that the prizes of earth were contemptible compared with the ultimate reward of God.

(3) The day came when Moses, because of his intervention on behalf of his people, had to leave Egypt and go to Midian (Exodus 2:14–22). Because of the order in which it comes, that must be what verse 27 refers to. Some people have found difficulty here, because the Exodus narrative says that it was because Moses feared Pharaoh that he fled to Midian (Exodus 2:14), while Hebrews says that he went out not fearing the blazing wrath of the king. There is no real contradiction. It is simply that the writer of the letter to the Hebrews saw even more deeply into the story. For Moses to go to Midian was not an act of fear; it was an act of courage. It showed the courage of the man who has learned to wait.

The Stoics were wise; they held that people should not throw their lives away by needlessly provoking the wrath of a tyrant. Seneca wrote: 'The wise man will never provoke the wrath of mighty men; nay, he will turn aside from it, in just the same way as sailors in sailing will not deliberately court the danger of the storm.' At that moment, Moses might have gone on – but his people were not ready. If he had gone on recklessly, he would simply have thrown his life away, and the deliverance from Egypt might never have happened. He was big enough and brave enough to wait until God said: 'Now is the hour.'

Moffatt quotes a saying of the biblical scholar A. S. Peake: 'The courage to abandon work on which one's heart is set and accept inaction cheerfully as the will of God is of the rarest and highest kind and can be created and sustained only by the clearest spiritual vision.' When our natural instincts say: 'Go on,' it takes a big and a brave person to wait. It is human to be afraid of missing the chance; but it is important to wait for the time of God – even when it seems like throwing a chance away.

(4) There came the day when Moses had to make all the arrangements for the first Passover. The account is in Exodus 12:12–48. The unleavened bread had to be made; the Passover lamb had to be slain; the doorpost had to be smeared with the blood of the lamb so that the Angel of Death would see the blood and pass over that house and not slay the first-born in it. But the really amazing thing is that, according to the Exodus story, Moses not only made these regulations for the night on which the children of Israel were leaving Israel; he also laid it down that *they were to be observed annually for all time*. That is to say, he never doubted the success of the enterprise, never doubted that the people would be delivered from Egypt and that some day they would reach the promised land. Here was a band of wretched Israelite slaves about to set off on a journey across an unknown desert to an unknown

promised land, and here was the whole power of Egypt hot upon their heels; yet Moses never doubted that God would bring them safely through. He was supremely the man who had the faith that, if God gave his people an order, he would also give them the strength to carry it out. Moses knew very well that God does not summon his servants to a difficult and challenging task and leave it at that; he goes with them every step of the way.

(5) There was the momentous act of the crossing of the Red Sea. The story is told in Exodus 14. There, we read of how the children of Israel were wondrously enabled to pass through and of how the Egyptians were engulfed when they tried to do the same. It was at that moment that the faith of Moses communicated itself to the people and drove them on when they might well have turned back. Here, we have the faith of a leader and of a people who were prepared to attempt the impossible at the command of God, realizing that the greatest barrier in the world is no barrier if God is there to help us to get over it. Moses possessed the faith to attempt what appeared to be the most insurmountable barriers, in the certainty that God would help the one who refused to turn back and insisted on going on.

Finally, this passage not only tells us of the faith of Moses; it also tells us of *the source of that faith*. Verse 27 tells us that he was able to face all things as one who sees the God who is invisible. The outstanding characteristic of Moses was the close intimacy of his relationship with God. In Exodus 33:9–11, we read of how he went into the tabernacle: 'Thus the Lord used to speak to Moses face to face, as one speaks to a friend.' In Numbers 12:7–8, we read of God's verdict on him when there were those who were ready to rebel against him: 'with him I speak face to face'. To put it simply: the secret of his faith was that Moses knew

God personally. To every task, he came out from God's presence.

It is told that, before a great battle, Napoleon would stand in his tent alone; he would send for his commanders to come to him, one by one; when they came in, he would say no word but would look them in the eye and shake them by the hand; and they would go out prepared to die for the general whom they loved. That is like Moses and God. Moses had the faith he had because he knew God in the way he did. When we come to it straight from God's presence, no task can ever defeat us. Our failure and our fear are so often due to the fact that we try to do things alone. The secret of victorious living is to face God before we face the world.

THE FAITH WHICH DEFIED THE FACTS

Hebrews 11:30-1

> It was by faith that the walls of Jericho fell down after they had been encircled for seven days. It was by faith that Rahab, the harlot, did not perish with the disobedient because she had welcomed the scouts in peace.

THE writer to the Hebrews has been citing as examples of faith the great figures of the time before Israel entered into the promised land. Now he takes two figures from the period of struggle when the children of Israel were winning a place for themselves within Palestine.

(1) The first is the story of the fall of Jericho. That strange old story is told in Joshua 6:1–20. Jericho was a strong fortified city with all gates barricaded. To take it seemed impossible. It was God's commandment that, once a day for six days, and in silence, the people should march round it,

led by seven priests marching in front of the ark and bearing trumpets of rams' horn. On the seventh day, the priests were to blow upon the trumpets, after the city had been encircled seven times, and the people were to shout with all their might, 'and the wall of the city will fall down flat'. As the old story tells it, so it happened.

That story left an indelible mark upon the memory of Israel. Centuries after this, Judas Maccabaeus and his men were facing the city of Caspis, so secure in its strength that its defenders laughed from their position of safety. 'But Judas and his men, calling upon the great Sovereign of the world, who without battering rams or engines of war overthrew Jericho in the days of Joshua, rushed furiously upon the walls. They took the city by the will of God' (2 Maccabees 12:15–16). The people never forgot what great things God had done for them; and, when some great effort was called for, they nerved themselves for it by remembering them.

Here is the very point the writer to the Hebrews wishes to make. The taking of Jericho was the result of an act of faith. It was taken by men who thought not of what they could do but of what God could do for them. They were prepared to believe that God could turn their obvious weakness into strength that could accomplish an incredible task. After the destruction of the Spanish Armada, there was erected on Plymouth Hoe a monument with the inscription: 'God sent his wind and they were scattered.' When the people of England saw how the storm and the gale had shattered the Spanish Armada, they said: 'God did it.' When we are faced with any great and demanding task, God is the ally we must never leave out of the reckoning. The things which we find it impossible to accomplish alone are always possible with God.

(2) The second story the writer to the Hebrews takes is that of Rahab. It is told in Joshua 2:1–21 and has its sequel in

Joshua 6:25. When Joshua sent out spies to spy out the situation in Jericho, they found a lodging in the house of Rahab, a prostitute. She protected them and enabled them to make their escape; and in return, when Jericho was taken, she and her family were saved from the general slaughter. It is extraordinary how Rahab became imprinted on the memory of Israel. James (2:25) quotes her as a great example of the good works which demonstrate faith. The Rabbis were proud to trace their ancestry to her. And, amazingly, she is one of the names which appear in the genealogy of Jesus (Matthew 1:5). The early Church father Clement of Rome quotes her as an outstanding example of one who was saved 'by faith and hospitality'.

When the writer to the Hebrews cites her as an example, the point he wants to make is this: Rahab, in the face of all the facts, believed in the God of Israel. She said to the spies whom she welcomed and hid: 'I know that the Lord has given you the land . . . The Lord your God is indeed God in heaven above and on earth below' (Joshua 2:9–11). At the moment when she was speaking, there seemed not one chance in a million that the children of Israel could capture Jericho. These nomads from the desert had no artillery and no siege-engines. Yet Rahab believed – and staked her whole future on the belief – that God would make the impossible possible. When common sense pronounced the situation hopeless, she had the uncommon sense to see beyond the situation. The real faith and the real courage are those which can take God's side when it seems doomed to defeat. As the hymn-writer F. W. Faber had it:

> Thrice blest is he to whom is given
> The instinct that can tell
> That God is on the field when he
> Is most invisible.

> For right is right, since God is God;
>   And right the day must win;
> To doubt would be disloyalty,
>   To falter would be sin.

Christians believe that no one who takes the side of God can ever ultimately be on the losing side – for, even if we experience earth's defeats, there is a victory whose trophies are in heaven.

THE HEROES OF THE FAITH

Hebrews 11:32–4

> And what more shall I say? Time will fail me if I try to recount the story of Gideon, of Barak, of Samson, of Jephthah, of David, of Samuel and of the prophets, men who, through faith, mastered kingdoms, did righteousness, obtained promises, shut the mouths of lions, quenched the power of fire, escaped the edge of the sword, from weakness were made strong, showed themselves strong in warfare, routed the ranks of aliens.

In this passage, the writer lets his mind's eye roam back over the history of his people; and from it he recalls a list of names of heroic individuals. He does not take them in any particular order; but, as we shall see when we look at the outstanding characteristics of each one individually, there is a line of thought which binds them all together.

The story of Gideon is told in Judges 6–7. With only 300 men, Gideon won a victory over the Ammonites in days when they had terrorized Israel, a victory which went ringing down the centuries. The story of Barak is in Judges 4–5. Under the inspiration of the prophetess Deborah, Barak assembled 10,000 young men and faced the fearful odds of the Canaanites with their 900 chariots of iron to win a quite incredible victory. It was as if a band of almost unarmed infantry had routed a division of tanks. The story of Samson is in Judges 13–16. Always, Samson was fighting alone. In the isolation of his splendid strength, again and again he faced the most amazing odds and emerged triumphant. He was the scourge of the Philistines. The story of Jephthah is in Judges 11–12. Jephthah was an illegitimate son; he was driven into a kind of exile and into the life of an outlaw; but, when the Israelites were living in fear of the Ammonites, the forgotten outlaw was called back and won a tremendous victory, although his vow to God cost him the life of his daughter. There was David, who had once been a shepherd boy and who, to his own and everyone else's astonishment, was anointed king in preference to all his brothers (1 Samuel 16:1–13). There was Samuel, born to his mother so late in life (1 Samuel 1), again and again moving alone as the only strong and faithful man of God among an easily frightened, discontented and rebellious people. There were the prophets, one after another bearing a faithful and isolated witness to God.

The whole list is made up of individuals who faced incredible odds for God. It cites people who never believed that God was on the side of the big battalions and who were willing to take tremendous and even terrifying risks for him – those who cheerfully and courageously and confidently accepted God-given tasks that, on human terms, were impossible. They were all individuals who were never afraid to stand alone and to face immense odds for the sake of their loyalty to God. The honour roll of history is of people who chose to be in God's minority rather than with the world's majority.

In the second part of the passage, the writer to the Hebrews tells what these remarkable individuals and others like them did, in a series of short, sharp phrases. For most of us, much of their impact may be lost, for this reason: *phrase after phrase is a reminiscence*. For those who knew the Scriptures well in their Greek version, phrase after phrase would ring a bell in the mind. The word used for *mastering kingdoms* is the word that Josephus, the Jewish historian, used of David. The phrase used for *did righteousness* is the description of David in 2 Samuel 8:15. The expression used for *shutting the mouths of lions* is that used of Daniel in Daniel 6:18, 23. The phrase about *quenching the power of fire* goes straight back to the story of Shadrach, Meshach and Abednego in Daniel 3:19–28. To speak about *escaping the edge of the sword* was to direct people's thoughts to the way in which Elijah escaped threatened assassination in 1 Kings 19:1ff., as did Elisha in 2 Kings 6:31ff. The trumpet-call about being *strong in warfare* and *routing the ranks of aliens* would immediately make people think of the unforgettable glories of the Maccabaean days.

The phrase about *being made strong out of weakness* might conjure up a number of pictures. It might paint the mental picture of the extraordinary healing of Hezekiah after he had turned his face to the wall to die (2 Kings 20:1–7). Perhaps more likely in the time in which the writer to the Hebrews wrote, it would remind his hearers of that epic but bloodthirsty incident told in the Book of Judith, one of the apocryphal books. There was a time when Israel was threatened by the armies of Nebuchadnezzar led by his general Holofernes. The Jewish town of Bethulia had determined to surrender in five days' time, for its supplies of food and water were at an end. In the town, there was a widow called Judith. She was wealthy and beautiful, but she had lived in lonely mourning since her husband Manasses had died. She dressed in all her finery, persuaded her people to let her out of the town and went is a struggle of which every Christian should know something; for, if in these times of bloodshed the Jews had surrendered their faith, Jesus could not have come. The story is like this.

About the year 170 BC, there was on the throne of Syria a king called Antiochus Epiphanes. He was a good governor, but he had an almost abnormal love for all things Greek, and saw himself as a missionary for the Greek way of life. He tried to introduce this into Palestine. He had some success; there were those who were willing to accept Greek culture, Greek drama and Greek athletics. Greek athletes trained naked, and some of the Jewish priests even went so far as to seek to obliterate the mark of circumcision from their bodies so that they might become Greek in every respect. So far, Antiochus had succeeded only in causing a division in the nation; the greater part of the Jews were unshakably true to their faith and could not be moved. Force and violence had not yet been used.

Then, in about 168 BC, the matter came to boiling point. Antiochus had an interest in Egypt. He gathered an army and invaded that country. To his deep humiliation, the Romans ordered him home. We have already seen just how this happened in our consideration of 3:1-6. To be told not to proceed with a campaign was a shattering blow to the pride of a king.

So, Antiochus turned for home, almost mad with rage; and on the way he turned aside and attacked Jerusalem, capturing it almost without an effort. It was said that 80,000 Jews were killed and 10,000 sold into captivity. But there was worse to come. He plundered the Temple. The golden altars of the shewbread and of the incense, the golden lamp stand, the golden vessels, even the curtains and the veils were taken. The treasury was ransacked and robbed. Even worse was to come. On the altar of the burnt offering, he offered sacrifices of pig's flesh to Zeus; and he turned the Temple chambers into brothels. No act of sacrilege was left out. Still worse was to come. He completely forbade circumcision and the possession of the Scriptures and of the law. He ordered the Jews to eat meats which were unclean and to sacrifice to the Greek gods. Inspectors went throughout the land to see that these orders were carried out. And if any were found to defy them, they 'underwent great miseries and bitter torments; for they were whipped with rods and their bodies were torn to pieces; they were crucified while they were still alive and breathed; they also strangled those women and their sons whom they had circumcised, as the king had appointed, hanging their sons about their necks as if they were upon their crosses. And if there were any sacred book of the law found, it was destroyed; and those with whom they were found miserably perished also' (Josephus, *Antiquities of the Jews*, 12:5:4). Never in all history has there been such a sadistic and deliberate attempt to wipe out a people's religion.

It is easy to see how this passage can be read against the terrible happenings of these days. The book of 4 Maccabees has two famous stories which were undoubtedly in the mind of the writer to the Hebrews when he made his list of the things that the people of faith have had to suffer.

The first is the story of Eleazar, the elderly priest (4 Maccabees 5–7). He was brought before Antiochus and ordered to eat pig's flesh, being threatened with the direst penalties if he refused. He did refuse. 'We, O Antiochus,' he said, 'who have been persuaded to govern our lives by the divine law, think that there is no compulsion more powerful than our obedience to the law.' He would not comply with the king's order, 'not even if you gouge out my eyes and burn my entrails'. They stripped him naked and flogged him with whips, while a herald stood by him, saying: 'Obey the king's commands.' His flesh was torn off by the whips, and he streamed down with blood, and his flanks were laid open by wounds. He collapsed, and one of the soldiers kicked him violently in the stomach to make him get up. In the end, even the guards were moved to amazed compassion. They suggested to him that they would bring him dressed meat which was not pork, and that he should eat it pretending that it was pork. He refused. 'We should now change our course and ourselves become a pattern of impiety to the young by setting them an example in the eating of defiling food.' In the end, they carried him to the fire and threw him on it, and 'burned him with maliciously contrived instruments, threw him down and poured stinking liquids into his nostrils'. So he died, declaring: 'I am dying by burning torments for the sake of the law.'

The second story is that of the seven brothers (4 Maccabees 8–14). They, too, were given the same choice and confronted with the same threats. They were confronted with 'wheels and joint-dislocators, rack and hooks and catapults and caldrons, braziers and thumb-screws and iron claws and wedges and bellows'. The first brother refused to eat the unclean things. They lashed him with whips and tied him to the wheel until he was dislocated and fractured in every limb. 'They spread fire under him, and while fanning the flames they tightened the wheel further. The wheel was completely smeared with blood, and the heap of coals was being quenched by the drippings of gore, and pieces of flesh were falling off the axles of the machine.' But he withstood their tortures and died faithful. The second brother they bound to the catapults. They put on spiked iron gloves. 'These leopard-like beasts tore out his sinews with the iron hands, flayed all his flesh up to his chin and tore away his scalp.' He, too, died faithful. The third brother was brought forward. Enraged by the man's boldness, the officers 'disjointed his hands and feet with their instruments, dismembering him by prying his limbs from their sockets and breaking his fingers and arms and legs and elbows'. In the end, they tore him apart on the catapult and flayed him alive. He, too, died faithful. They cut out the tongue of the fourth brother before they submitted him to similar tortures. The fifth brother they bound to the wheel, bending his body round the edge of it, and then fastened him with iron fetters to the catapult and tore him in pieces. The sixth they broke upon the wheel 'and he was roasted from underneath. To his back they applied sharp spits that had been heated in the fire, and pierced his ribs so that his entrails were burned through.' The seventh brother they roasted alive in a gigantic brazier. These, too, died faithful.

These are the things of which the writer to the Hebrews is thinking; and these are things which we do well also to remember. It was due to the faith of these men that the Jewish religion was not completely destroyed. If that religion had been destroyed, what would have happened to the purposes of God? How could Jesus have been born into the world if Judaism had ceased to exist? In a very real way, we owe our Christianity to these martyrs of the times when Antiochus made his deliberate attempt to wipe out the Jewish religion.

The day came when the situation ignited. The agents of Antiochus had gone to a town called Modein and had erected an altar there to make the inhabitants sacrifice to the Greek gods. The emissaries of Antiochus tried to persuade a certain Mattathias to set an example by offering sacrifice, for he was a distinguished and influential man. He refused in anger. But another Jew, seeking to gain approval and to save his own life, came forward and was about to sacrifice.

Mattathias, moved to uncontrollable wrath, seized a sword and killed his faithless countryman and the king's commissioner with him.

The signal for rebellion had been given. Mattathias and his sons and other like-minded people took to the hills; and once again the phrases used to describe their life there were in the mind of the writer to the Hebrews, and he has echoes of them over and over again. 'Then he [Mattathias] and his sons fled to the hills and left all that they had in the town' (1 Maccabees 2:28). 'Judas Maccabaeus, with about nine others, got away to the wilderness and kept himself and his companions alive in the mountains as wild animals do' (2 Maccabees 5:27). 'Others, who had assembled in the caves nearby, in order to observe the seventh day secretly, were betrayed . . . were all burned together' (2 Maccabees 6:11). 'They had been wandering in the mountains and caves like wild animals' (2 Maccabees 10:6). In the end, under Judas Maccabaeus and his brothers, the Jews regained their freedom, the Temple was cleansed and the faith flourished again.

In this passage, the writer to the Hebrews has done the same as before. He does not actually mention these things. Far better that his readers should be moved by a phrase here and there to remember them for themselves.

In the end, he says something. All these died before the final unfolding of God's promise and the coming of his Messiah into the world. It was as if God had arranged things in such a way that the full blaze of his glory should not be revealed until we and they could enjoy it together. The writer to the Hebrews is saying: 'See! the glory of God has come. But see what it cost to make it possible! That is the faith which gave you your religion. What can you do except be true to a heritage like that?'

THE RACE AND THE GOAL

Hebrews 12:1–2

> Therefore, since we have so great a cloud of witnesses
> enveloping us, let us strip off every weight and let us
> rid ourselves of the sin which so persistently surrounds
> us, and let us run with steadfast endurance the course
> that is marked out for us and, as we do so, let us keep
> our gaze fixed on Jesus who, in order to win the joy that
> was set before him, steadfastly endured the cross,
> thinking nothing of its shame, and has now taken his
> seat at the right hand of the throne of God.

THIS is one of the great, moving passages of the New Testament; and in it the writer has given us a near-perfect summary of the Christian life.

(1) In the Christian life, we have *a goal*. Christians are not people who stroll along the byways of life in a completely unconcerned manner; they travel on the high road. They are not tourists, who return each night to the place from which they started; they are pilgrims who are always travelling on the way. The goal is nothing less than the likeness of Christ. The Christian life is going somewhere, and at each day's ending we would do well to ask ourselves: 'Am I any further on?'

(2) In the Christian life, we have *an inspiration*. We have the thought of the unseen cloud of witnesses; and they are witnesses in a double sense, for they have witnessed their confession to Christ and they are now witnesses of our performance. Christians are like runners in some crowded stadium. As they press on, the crowd looks down; and the crowd looking down are those who have already won the crown.

The first-century writer Pseudo-Longinus, in his great work *On the Sublime*, has a recipe for greatness in literary endeavour. 'It is a good thing', he writes, 'to form the question in our souls, "How would Homer perhaps have said this? How would Plato or Demosthenes have lifted it up to sublimity? How would Thucydides have put it in his history?" For when the faces of these people come before us in our emulation, they will, as it were, illumine our road and will lift us up to those standards of perfection which we have imagined in our minds. It would be still better if we were to suggest this to our minds, "What would this that I have said sound like to Homer, if he were standing by, or to Demosthenes, or how would they have reacted to it?" In truth it is a supreme test to imagine such a judgment court and theatre for our own private productions, and, in imagination, to submit an account of our writings to such heroes as judges.'

Actors would act with increased intensity if they knew that one of the greatest of their profession was sitting in the stalls watching them. Athletes would double their efforts if they knew that the stadium was full of famous Olympic athletes watching their performance. It is of the very essence of the Christian life that it is lived in the gaze of the heroes of the faith who lived, suffered and died in their day and generation. How can anyone avoid the struggle for greatness when an audience like that is looking down on us?

(3) In the Christian life, we have *a handicap*. If we are encircled by the greatness of the past, we are also encircled by the handicap of our own sin. No one would attempt to climb Mount Everest weighed down with a whole load of unnecessary baggage. If we want to travel far, we must travel light. There is in life an essential duty to discard things. There may be habits, pleasures, self-indulgences or associations which hold us back. We must shed them as athletes take off their tracksuits when they go to the starting blocks; and often we will need the help of Christ to enable us to do so.

(4) In the Christian life, we have *a means*. That means is *steadfast endurance*. The word is *hupomonē*, which means not the patience which sits down and accepts things but the patience which takes charge of them. It is not some romantic notion which lends us wings to fly over the difficulties and the hard places. It is a determination, unhurrying and yet undelaying, which goes steadily on and refuses to be deflected. Obstacles do not daunt it and discouragements do not take its hope away. It is the steadfast endurance which carries on until, in the end, it gets there.

(5) In the Christian life, we have *an example*. That example is Jesus himself. For the goal that was set before him, he endured all things; to win it meant the way of the cross. The writer to the Hebrews has a flash of insight – *despising the shame*, he says. Jesus was sensitive; never had any individual so sensitive a heart. A cross was a humiliating thing. It was for criminals, for those whom society regarded as the dregs of humanity – and yet he accepted it. The sixteenth-century saint Philip of Neri encourages us 'to despise the world, to despise ourselves, and to despise the fact that we are despised' (*spernere mundum, spernere te ipsum, spernere te sperni*). If Jesus could endure like that, so must we.

(6) In the Christian life, we have *a presence*, the presence of Jesus. He is both the goal of our journey and the companion of our way; at the same time, the one whom we go to meet and the one with whom we travel. The wonder of the Christian life is that we press on surrounded by the saints, oblivious to everything but the glory of the goal and always in the company of the one who has already made the journey and reached the goal, and who waits to welcome us when we reach the end.

THE STANDARD OF COMPARISON

Hebrews 12:3-4

> Consider him who steadfastly endured such opposition
> at the hands of sinners, and compare your lives with
> his, so that you may not faint and grow weary in your
> souls. You have not yet had to resist to the point of
> blood in your struggle against sin.

THE writer to the Hebrews uses two very vivid words when
he speaks of *fainting* and *growing weary*. They are the words
which Aristotle uses of an athlete who flings himself on the
ground in a state of collapse *after* he has surged past the
winning post of the race. So, this passage is in effect saying:
'Don't give up too soon; don't collapse until the winning
post is passed.'

To urge his readers to that, the writer uses two arguments.

(1) For them, the struggle of Christianity has not yet
become a mortal struggle. When he speaks of resisting to the
point of blood, he uses the very phrase used by the
Maccabaean leaders when they called on their troops to fight
to the death. When the writer to the Hebrews says that his
people have not yet resisted to the point of blood, as James
Moffatt puts it, 'he is not blaming them, he is *shaming* them'.
When they think of what the heroes of the past went through
to make their faith possible, surely they cannot drift into
lethargy or flinch from conflict.

(2) He pleads with them to compare what they have to
suffer with what Jesus suffered. He gave up the glory which
was his; he came into all the narrowness of the life of
humanity; he faced hostility; in the end, he had to die upon a
cross. So, the writer to the Hebrews in effect demands: 'How
can you compare what you have to go through with what he

went through? He did all that for you – what are you going to do for him?'

These two verses stress the essential costliness of Christian faith. It cost the lives of the martyrs; it cost the life of the one who was the Son of God. A thing which cost so much cannot be discarded lightly. A heritage like that is not something that can be handed down tarnished. These two verses make the demand that comes to every Christian: 'Show yourself worthy of the sacrifice that others and God have made for you.'

THE DISCIPLINE OF GOD

Hebrews 12:5–11

Have you forgotten the appeal, an appeal which reasons with you as sons?

'My son, do not treat lightly the discipline which the Lord sends;

Never lose heart when you are put to the test by him;

For the Lord disciplines the man whom he loves, and scourges every son whom he receives.'

It is for the sake of discipline that you must endure. It is because he is treating us as sons that God sends these things upon us. What son is there whom his father does not discipline? If you are left without discipline – that discipline which everyone must share – then you are bastards and not sons. Surely it is true that we have human fathers who discipline us, and we pay heed to them. Surely we are still more bound to submit to the Father of the spirits of men, for that is the only way in which we can find real life. It was only for a short time that our human fathers disciplined us, and they did it as they thought best; but God disciplines us for our highest

good, and he does so to make us fit to share his own
holiness. No discipline seems to be a thing of joy when
we are actually undergoing it, but afterwards it yields a
fruit which is all to our highest welfare – the fruit of a
righteous life – to those who are trained by it.

THE writer to the Hebrews sets out yet another reason why
people should cheerfully bear affliction when it comes to
them. He has urged them to bear it because the great saints of
the past have borne it. He has urged them to bear it because
anything they may have to bear is as nothing compared with
what Jesus Christ had to bear. Now he says that they must
bear hardship because it is sent as a discipline from God, and
no life can have any value without discipline.

Parents always discipline their children. It would not be a
mark of love to let children do what they like and have nothing
but an easy way; it would show that the parents regarded the
children as illegitimate children to whom they felt neither
love nor responsibility. We submit to the discipline of earthly
parents, which is imposed only for a short time until we reach
years of maturity, and which at best always contains an
element of arbitrariness. We owe our physical existence to
our human parents; how much more should we submit to the
discipline of God to whom we owe our immortal spirits and
who, in his wisdom, seeks for nothing but our highest good?

There is a curious passage in Xenophon's *Cyropaedia*.
There is an argument about whether the person who makes
people laugh or the one who makes them weep is of most use
in the world. Aglaitidas says: 'He that makes his friends laugh
seems to me to do them much less service than he who makes
them weep; and, if you will look at it rightly, you, too, will
find that I speak the truth. At any rate, fathers develop
self-control in their sons by making them weep, and teachers
impress good lessons on their pupils in the same way, and

laws, too, turn the citizens to justice by making them weep. But could you say that those who make us laugh either do good to our bodies or make our minds any more fitted for the management of our private business or the affairs of state?' It was the view of Aglaitidas that it was the person who exerted discipline who really did good to others.

There is no doubt that this passage would come to those who heard it for the first time with a double impact, for the whole world knew of that amazing thing the *patria potestas*, the father's power. By law, a Roman father had absolute power over his family. If his son married, the father continued to have absolute power over both him and any grandchildren there might be. It began at the moment of birth. A Roman father could keep or discard his new-born child as he liked. He could bind or beat his son; he could sell him into slavery; and he even had the right to execute him. True, when a father was about to take serious steps against a member of his family, he usually called a council of all its adult male members; but he did not need to. True, in later years, public opinion would not permit the execution of a son by a father; but it happened as late as the time of Augustus. Sallust, the Roman historian, tells us of an incident during the Catiline conspiracy. Catiline rebelled against Rome, and among those who went out to join his forces was Aulus Fulvius, the son of a Roman senator. He was arrested and brought back, and his own father tried him and judged him and ordered him to be put to death. In regard to the *patria potestas*, a Roman son never came of age. He might have engaged on a state career; he might be holding the highest rank of magistrate; he might be held in honour by the whole country. All that did not matter; he was directly and completely under his father's power as long as his father lived. If ever a people knew what parental discipline was, the Romans did; and when the writer to the Hebrews talked about the way in which a human father disciplined his son, his readers knew very well what he was talking about.

So, the writer insists that we must look on all the hardships of life as the discipline of God and as sent to work not for our harm but for our ultimate and highest good. To prove his point, he quotes Proverbs 3:11–12. There are many ways in which people look at the discipline which God sends.

(1) They may resign themselves to it and *accept* it. That is what the Stoics did. They held that nothing in this world happens outside the will of God; therefore, they argued, there is nothing to do but to accept it. To do anything else is simply to batter one's head against the walls of the universe. That is possibly the acceptance of supreme wisdom; but nonetheless it is the acceptance not of a parent's love but of a parent's power. It is not a willing but a defeated acceptance.

(2) People may accept discipline *with the grim sense of getting it over as soon as possible*. A certain famous Roman said: 'I will let nothing interrupt my life.' To accept discipline like that is to regard it as something that is inflicted on us which is to be struggled through with defiance and certainly not with gratitude.

(3) People may accept discipline *with the self-pity which leads in the end to collapse*. Some people, when they are caught up in a difficult situation, give the impression that they are the only people in the world whom life ever hurt. They are lost in their self-pity.

(4) People may accept discipline *as a punishment which they resent*. It is strange that, at this time, the Romans saw in national and personal disasters nothing but the vengeance of the gods. Lucan the poet wrote: 'Happy were Rome indeed, and blessed citizens would she have, if the gods were as much concerned with caring for men as they are with exacting vengeance from them.' The historian Tacitus held that the

disasters of the nation were proof that the interest of the gods lay not in people's safety but in their punishment. There are still people who regard God as vindictive. When something happens to them or to those whom they love, their question is: 'What did I do to deserve this?' And the question is asked in such a tone as to make it clear that they regard the whole matter as an unjust punishment from God. It never dawns upon them to ask: 'What is God trying to teach me and to do with me through this experience?'

(5) So we come to the last attitude. People may accept discipline *as coming from a loving father*. The fourth-century biblical scholar Jerome said a paradoxical but true thing: 'The greatest anger of all is when God is no longer angry with us when we sin.' He meant that the supreme punishment is when God leaves us alone as unteachable. Christians know that 'a father's hand will never cause his child a needless tear' and that everything can be utilized to make us wiser and better men and women. As Robert Browning wrote in 'Rabbi ben Ezra':

> Then welcome each rebuff
> That turns earth's smoothness rough,
> Each sting that bids nor sit nor stand but go!
> Be our joy three-parts pain!
> Strive and hold cheap the strain;
> Learn, nor account the pang; dare, never grudge the throe!
>
> For thence – a paradox
> Which comforts while it mocks –
> Shall life succeed in that it seems to fail;
> What I aspired to be,
> And was not, comforts me.
> A brute I might have been, but would not sink i' the scale.

We shall stop feeling self-pity and resentment and end our rebellious complaining if we remember that there is no discipline of God which does not arise out of love and is not aimed at good.

DUTIES, AIMS AND DANGERS

Hebrews 12:12–17

So, then, lift up the slack hands. Strengthen the weak knees. And make straight the paths of your feet so that the bones of the lame may not be completely dislocated but rather may be cured. Make peace your aim – and do it all together – and aim at that holiness without which no one can see the Lord. Watch that no one misses the grace of God. Watch that no pernicious influence grows up to involve you in troubles. And watch that the main body of your people are not soiled by any such thing. Watch that no one falls into sexual impurity or turns to an unhallowed life, as Esau did, Esau who, for a single meal, gave away his birthright. For you are well aware of how when he afterwards wanted to claim the blessing he ought to have inherited, he was rejected – for he had no opportunity to change his mind – although he sought that blessing with tears.

WITH this passage, the writer to the Hebrews comes to the problems of everyday Christian life and living. He knew that sometimes it is given to us to rise up with inspiration as if we had the wings of eagles; he knew that sometimes we are able to run and not grow weary in the pursuit of some great moment of endeavour; but he also knew that, of all things, it is hardest to continue to walk day after day and not to faint. Here, he is thinking of the daily struggle of the Christian way.

(1) He begins by reminding them of their *duties*. In every congregation and in every Christian society, there are those who are weaker and more likely to go astray and to abandon the struggle. It is the duty of those who are stronger to put fresh vigour into listless hands and fresh strength into failing feet. The phrase used for *slack hands* is the same as is used to describe the children of Israel in the days when they wanted to abandon the harsh demands of the journey across the wilderness and to return to the ease and the fleshpots of Egypt.

The Odes of Solomon (6:14ff.) have a description of the work of those who are true servants and ministers:

> They have refreshed the dry lips,
> And have raised up the will that was paralysed . . .
> And limbs that were fallen
> They have straightened and raised up.

One of life's greatest glories is to be an encourager of those who are near to despair and a strengthener of those whose strength is failing. To help these people, we have, as the writer to the Hebrews puts it, 'to make their paths straight'. Christians have a double duty; they have a duty to God and a duty to other people. The Testament of Simeon (5:2–3) has an illuminating description of the duty of those who would strive for goodness. 'Make your heart good in the sight of the Lord; and make your ways straight in the sight of men; so you will find favour in the sight of the Lord and of men.'

To God, individuals must present a clean heart; to others, they must present an upright life. To show others the right way to walk, by personal example to keep them on the right road, to remove from the path something that would make them stumble, to make the journey easier for faltering and lagging feet, is a Christian duty. Christians must offer their hearts to God and their service and example to their neighbours.

(2) The writer to the Hebrews turns to the *aims* which must always guide Christians.

(a) They must aim at *peace*. In Jewish thought and language, peace was not a negative thing; it was intensely positive. It was not simply freedom from trouble; it was two things.

First, it was everything which makes for a person's highest good. As the Jews saw it, that highest good was to be found in obedience to God. In the Authorized Version, Proverbs says: 'My son, forget not my law; but let thine heart keep my commandments: for length of days and long life and *peace* shall they add unto thee' (3:1–2). Christians must aim at that complete obedience to God in which life finds its highest happiness, its greatest good, its perfect consummation, its *peace*. Second, *peace* meant right relationships between individuals. It meant a state when hatred was banished and people sought nothing but the good of their neighbours. The writer to the Hebrews says: 'Seek to live together as Christian men and women ought to live, in the real unity which comes from living in Christ.'

The peace to be sought is that coming from obedience to God's will, which raises life to its highest fulfilment and enables us to live in and to produce right relationships with one another.

One thing remains to be noted: that kind of peace is to be *pursued*. It requires an effort; it is not something which just happens. It is the product of mental and spiritual toil and sweat. In 'The Glory of the Garden', Rudyard Kipling wrote:

Our England is a garden, and such gardens are not made
By singing:– 'Oh, how beautiful!' and sitting in the
    shade,

While better men than we go out and start their
   working-lives
At grubbing weeds from gravel-paths with broken
   dinner-knives.

The gifts of God are given, but they are not given away; they have to be *won*, for they can be received only on God's conditions – and the supreme condition is obedience to himself.

(b) They must aim at *holiness* (*hagiasmos*). *Hagiasmos* has in it the same root as the adjective *hagios*, which is usually translated as *holy*. The root meaning is always *difference* and *separation*. Although living in the world, the person who is *hagios* must always in one sense be different from it and separate from it. The standards of such people are not the world's standards, nor is their conduct the world's conduct. Their aim is not to be in good standing with others but to be in good standing with God. *Hagiasmos*, as B. F. Westcott put it, is 'the preparation for the presence of God'. The Christian life is dominated by the constant memory that its greatest aim is to enter into the presence of God.

(3) The writer to the Hebrews goes on to indicate the *dangers* which threaten the Christian life.

(a) There is the danger of *missing the grace of God*. The word he uses might be paraphrased as *failing to keep up with the grace of God*. The early Greek commentator Theophylact interprets this in terms of a journey of a band of travellers who every now and again check up: 'Has anyone fallen out? Has anyone been left behind while the others have pressed on?' In Micah, there is a vivid text (4:6): 'I will assemble the lame.' James Moffatt translates it: 'I will collect the stragglers.' It is easy to straggle away, to linger behind, to drift instead of to press on, and so to miss the grace of God. There is no opportunity in this life which cannot be missed.

The grace of God brings to us the opportunity to make ourselves and to make life what they are meant to be. Anyone may, through lethargy, thoughtlessness, unawareness or by putting things off, miss the chances which grace brings. We must always be on the look-out against that.

(b) There is the danger of what the Revised Standard Version calls 'a root bearing poisonous and bitter fruit'. The phrase comes from Deuteronomy 29:18; and there it describes the person who follows strange gods and encourages others to do so, and who thereby becomes a destructive influence on the life of the community. The writer to the Hebrews is warning against those who are a corrupting influence. There are always those who think that Christian standards are unnecessarily strict and fussy; there are always those who do not see why they should not accept the world's standards of life and conduct. This was especially so in the early Church. It was a little island of Christianity surrounded by a sea of paganism; its members were, at most, only one generation away from paganism. It was easy to lapse into the old standards. This is a warning against the infection of the world, sometimes deliberately, sometimes unconsciously, spread within the Christian society.

(c) There is the danger of *falling into immorality or lapsing into an unhallowed life*. The word used for *unhallowed* is *bebēlos*. It has an interesting background that sheds light on its meaning. It was used for ground that was *profane* as distinct from ground that was *consecrated*. The ancient world had its religions into which only the initiated could come. *Bebēlos* was used for the person who was *uninitiated* and *uninterested* as opposed to the person who was *devout*. It was applied to people like Antiochus Epiphanes who were determined to wipe out all true religion; it was applied to Jews who had given up their beliefs and had forsaken God. B. F. Westcott sums up this word by saying that it describes someone whose mind recognizes nothing higher than earth, for whom there is nothing sacred, who has no reverence for the unseen. An *unhallowed* life is a life without any awareness of or interest in God. In its thoughts, aims and pleasures, it is completely earthbound. We must always take care that we do not drift into a frame of mind and heart which has no horizon beyond this world.

To sum it all up, the writer to the Hebrews cites the example of Esau. He really puts two stories together – Genesis 25:28–34 and Genesis 27:1–39. In the first, Esau came in from the field ravenously hungry and sold his birthright to Jacob for a share of the food which he was preparing. The second story tells how Jacob subtly robbed Esau of his birthright by impersonating him when Isaac was old and blind, and so gained the blessing which belonged to Esau as the elder of the two sons. It was when Esau sought the blessing that Jacob had shrewdly obtained and learned he could not get it that he lifted up his voice and wept (Genesis 27:38).

There is more to this than lies upon the surface. In Jewish legend and in Rabbinic elaboration, Esau had come to be looked upon as the entirely sensual man, the man who put the needs of his body first. Jewish legend says that while Jacob and Esau – they were twins – were still in their mother's womb, Jacob said to Esau: 'My brother, there are two worlds before us, this world and the world to come. In this world, men eat and drink and traffic and marry and bring up sons and daughters; but all this does not take place in the world to come. If you like, take this world and I will take the other.' And Esau was well content to take this world, because he did not believe that there was any other. On that very day when Jacob's deception gained him Isaac's blessing, legend said that Esau had already committed five sins: 'he had worshipped with strange worship, he had shed innocent blood, he had pursued a betrothed damsel, he had denied the life of the world to come, and he had despised his birthright'.

Jewish interpretation saw Esau as the sensual man, the man who saw no pleasures beyond the crude pleasures of this world. People like that sell their birthright; for they throw away their inheritance when they throw away eternity.

The writer to the Hebrews says, according to the Authorized Version, that Esau *found no place for repentance*. The Greek for repentance is *metanoia*, which literally means *a change of mind*. It is better to say that it was now impossible for Esau to change his mind. It is not that he was barred from the forgiveness of God. It is just the grim fact that there are certain choices which cannot be unmade and certain consequences which not even God can take away. Once a choice has been made, it stands. God can and will forgive, but he cannot turn back the clock.

We do well to remember that there is a certain finality in life. If, like Esau, we take the way of this world and make physical things our ultimate good, if we choose the pleasures of the present in preference to the joys of eternity, God can and will still forgive; but something has happened that can never be undone. There are certain things in which we cannot change our minds but must live our lives by the choice that we have made.

THE TERROR OF THE OLD
AND THE GLORY OF THE NEW

Hebrews 12:18–24

It is not to something that can be touched that you have come, to a flaming fire, to mist and gloom and storm

blast, and to the blare of a trumpet, and to a voice which
spoke such words that those who heard it begged that
not another word should be further spoken unto them,
for they could not bear the command: 'If even a beast
touches the mountain, it shall be stoned.' So terrifying
was the apparition that Moses said: 'I am in utter fear
and trembling.' But you have come to Mount Sion and
to the city of the living God, the heavenly Jerusalem, to
ten thousands of angels gathered in glad assembly, to
the assembly of the honoured ones whose names are in
the registers of heaven, to that God who is judge of all,
to the spirits of just men who have come to that goal for
which they were created, and to Jesus, the mediator of
the new covenant, to the sprinkled blood which has a
message greater than the blood of Abel.

THIS passage is a contrast between the old and the new. It is a
contrast between the giving of the law on Mount Sinai and
the new covenant of which Jesus is the mediator. Down to
verse 21, it has echo after echo of the story of the giving of
the law on Mount Sinai. Deuteronomy 4:11 describes that
first law-giving: 'you approached and stood at the foot of the
mountain while the mountain was blazing up to the very
heavens, shrouded in dark clouds. Then the Lord spoke to
you out of the fire.' Exodus 19:12–13 tells of the unapproachability of that awful mountain: 'You shall set limits for the
people all around, saying, "Be careful not to go up to the
mountain or to touch the edge of it. Any who touch the
mountain shall be put to death. No hand shall touch them,
but they shall be stoned or shot with arrows; whether animal
or human being, they shall not live." When the trumpet sounds
a long blast, they may go up on the mountain.' Deuteronomy
5:23–7 tells how the people were so afraid to hear the voice
of God for themselves that they asked Moses to go and to

bring God's message to them. 'If we hear the voice of the Lord our God any longer, we shall die.' Deuteronomy 9:19 tells of the terror of Moses, but the writer to the Hebrews has transferred these words to the giving of the law, although in the original story they were spoken by Moses when he came down from the mountain and found the people worshipping the golden calf. The whole passage down to verse 21 is a string of reminiscences from the story of the giving of the law at Mount Sinai. All the terrifying things have been gathered together to stress the awfulness of that scene.

In the giving of the law at Mount Sinai, three things are stressed. (1) *The sheer majesty of God*. The story stresses the shattering power of God, and in it there is no love at all. (2) *The absolute unapproachability of God*. Far from the way being open to God, anyone who tries to approach him meets death. (3) *The sheer terror of God*. Here is nothing but an awe-stricken fear which is afraid to look and even to listen.

Then at verse 22 comes the difference. The first section deals with all that can be expected under the old covenant – a God of lonely majesty, complete separation from men and women, and overwhelming fear. But to Christians has come the new covenant and a new relationship with God.

The writer to the Hebrews makes a list of the new glories that await Christians.

(1) The new Jerusalem awaits them. This world with all its impermanence, its fears, its mysteries and its separations goes, and life for Christians is made new.

(2) The angels await them in joyful assembly. The word used for *joyful assembly* is *panēguris*, which is the word for a joyful national assembly in honour of the gods. To the Greeks, it described a joyful holy day when everyone rejoiced. For Christians, the joy of heaven is such that it makes even the angels break into rejoicing.

(3) God's elected people await them. The writer to the Hebrews uses two words to describe these people. He says literally that they are *the first-born*. Now, the characteristic of the *first-born* son is that the inheritance and the honour are his. He says that they are those whose *names are written in the registers of heaven*. In ancient times, kings kept a register of their faithful citizens. So, those who await the Christians are all whom God has honoured and all whom God has reckoned among his faithful citizens.

(4) God the Judge awaits them. The writer to the Hebrews never forgot that, at the end, Christians must stand the scrutiny of God. The glory is there; but the awe and the fear of God still remain. The New Testament is never in the slightest danger of sentimentalizing the idea of God.

(5) The spirits of all good men and women who have achieved their goal await them. Once they encircled them in the unseen cloud; now Christians will be part of that company. They go to join those whose names are on God's roll of honour.

(6) Finally, the writer to the Hebrews says that it was Jesus who initiated this new covenant and made this new relationship with God possible. It was he, the perfect priest and the perfect sacrifice, who made the unapproachable approachable; and he did this at the cost of his blood. So, the section ends with a curious contrast between the blood of Abel and the blood of Jesus. When Abel was slain, his blood upon the ground called for vengeance (Genesis 4:10); but, when Jesus was slain, his blood opened up the way of reconciliation. His sacrifice made it possible for us to be friends with God.

Once, human beings were under the terror of the law; the relationship between them and God was one of unbridgeable distance and shuddering fear. But after Jesus came and lived and died, the God who was distant and unapproachable was brought near, and the way opened to his presence.

THE GREATER OBLIGATION

Hebrews 12:25-9

> See that you do not refuse to listen to his voice; for if they who refused to listen to the one who brought the oracles of God upon earth did not escape, how much more shall we not escape if we turn away from him who speaks from heaven? Then his voice shook the earth but now the voice of the promise is: 'Still once more I will shake not only the earth but heaven also.' That phrase 'still once more' signifies the removal of the things that are shaken, because they are merely created things, in order that the things which cannot be shaken may remain. Therefore let us give thanks because we are receiving a kingdom that cannot be shaken, a kingdom in which we must worship God acceptably, with reverence and with fear, for our God, too, is a consuming fire.

HERE, the writer begins with a contrast which is also a warning. Moses brought to earth the oracles of God. The word that he uses (*chrēmatizein*) implies that Moses was only the *transmitter* of these oracles, the mouthpiece through which God spoke; and yet anyone who broke these commandments did not escape punishment. On the other hand, there is Jesus. The word used of him (*lalein*) implies the direct speech of God. He was not merely the transmitter of God's voice, he *was* God's voice. If that is so, how much more will someone who refuses to obey him find punishment? If someone deserves to be condemned for neglecting the imperfect message of the law, how much more does that person deserve to be condemned for neglecting the perfect message of the gospel? Because the gospel is the full revelation of God, there is laid on those who hear it a double and a terrible responsibility; and their condemnation must be all the more if they neglect it.

The writer to the Hebrews goes on to draw out another thought. When the law was given, the earth was shaken. 'Now Mount Sinai was wrapped in smoke, because the Lord had descended upon it in fire; the smoke went up like the smoke of a kiln, while the whole mountain shook violently' (Exodus 19:18). 'Tremble, O earth, at the presence of the Lord' (Psalm 114:7). 'The earth quaked, the heavens poured down rain at the presence of God' (Psalm 68:8). 'The crash of your thunder was in the whirlwind; your lightnings lit up the world; the earth trembled and shook' (Psalm 77:18).

The writer to the Hebrews finds another reference to the shaking of the earth in Haggai 2:6. There, the Greek version of the Old Testament says: 'Once again, in a little while [the Hebrew says "very soon"], I will shake the heavens and the earth and the sea and the dry land.' The writer to the Hebrews takes this to be an announcement of the day when this earth shall pass away and the new age will begin. In that day, everything that can be shaken will be destroyed; the only things to remain will be the things which can never be shaken; and chief among them is our relationship with God.

All things may pass away; the world as we know it may be uprooted; life as we experience it may come to an end; but one thing stands eternally sure – the relationship of every Christian to God.

If that is so, there is a great obligation laid upon us. We must worship God with reverence and serve him with fear; for nothing must be allowed to disturb that relationship which will be our salvation when the world passes away. So, the writer to the Hebrews finishes with one of those threatening quotations which he so often flings like a thunderbolt at his readers. It is a quotation from Deuteronomy 4:24. Moses is telling the people that they must never break their agreement with God and lapse into idolatry, for he is a jealous God. They must worship only him, or they will find that he is a consuming fire. It is as if the writer to the Hebrews was saying: 'There is a choice before you. Remain steadfastly true to God, and in the day when the universe is shaken into destruction your relationship with him will stand safe and secure. Be false to him, and the God who might have been your salvation will be to you a consuming fire of destruction.' It is a grim thought; but in it there is the eternal truth that, if we are true to God, we gain everything; and, if we are untrue to God, we lose everything. In this present time and in eternity, nothing really matters except loyalty to God.

THE MARKS OF THE CHRISTIAN LIFE

Hebrews 13:1-6

Let brotherly love be always with you.

Do not forget the duty of hospitality for, in remembering this duty, there are some who have entertained angels without knowing that they were doing so.

Remember those who are in prison, for you yourselves know what it is like to be a prisoner; remember those who are suffering ill-treatment, for the same thing can happen to you so long as you are in the body.

Let marriage be held in honour among you all, and never let the marriage bed be defiled. God judges those who are adulterers and immoral in their conduct.

> Let your way of life be free from the love of money.
> Be content with what you have, for he has said: 'I will
> never fail you and I will never forsake you'; so that we
> can say with confidence: 'The Lord is my helper: I will
> not be afraid. What can man do to me?'

As he comes to the close of the letter, the writer to the
Hebrews turns to practical things. Here, he outlines five
essential qualities of the Christian life.

(1) There is *brotherly or mutual love*. The very circumstances of the early Church sometimes threatened love within
the community. The very fact that they took their religion as
seriously as they did was in one sense a danger. In a church
which is threatened from the outside and desperately in
earnest on the inside, there are always two dangers. First,
there is the danger of heresy-hunting. The very desire to keep
the faith pure tends to make people eager to track down and
eliminate the heretic and the person whose faith has gone
astray. Second, there is the danger of stern and unsympathetic
treatment of those whose nerve and faith have failed. The
very necessity of unswerving loyalty in a hostile pagan world
tends to make more rigorous the treatment of any who in
some crisis did not have the courage to stand up for their
faith. It is a great thing to keep the faith pure; but, when the
desire to do so makes us censorious, harsh and unsympathetic,
mutual love is destroyed, and we are left with a situation
which may be worse than the one we tried to avoid. Somehow
or other, we have to combine two things – an earnestness in
the faith and a kindness to those who have strayed from it.

(2) There is *hospitality*. The ancient world loved and
honoured hospitality. The Jews listed six things which were
important both in this life and for the life to come, and the
list begins: 'Hospitality to the stranger and visiting the sick.'
The Greeks gave Zeus, as one of his favourite titles, the title

Zeus Xenios, which means Zeus, the god of strangers. The traveller and the stranger were under the protection of the king of the gods. Hospitality, as James Moffatt says, was a very important aspect of ancient religion.

Inns were filthy and ruinously expensive, and had a bad reputation. The Greeks always had a dislike of hospitality given for money; innkeeping seemed to them an unnatural business. In *The Frogs* by Aristophanes, Dionysus asks Heracles, when they are discussing finding a lodging, if he knows where there are fewest fleas. Plato in *The Laws* speaks of the innkeeper holding travellers to ransom. It is not without significance that Josephus says that Rahab, the prostitute who sheltered Joshua's scouts in Jericho, kept an inn. When Theophrastus wrote his character sketch of the reckless man, he said that he was fit to keep an inn or run a brothel; he put both occupations on the same level.

In the ancient world, there was a rather wonderful system of what were called 'guest friendships'. Throughout the years, families, even when they had lost active touch with each other, had an arrangement that, whenever it was needed, they would make accommodation available for each other. This hospitality was even more necessary among Christians. Slaves had no home of their own to go to. Wandering preachers and prophets were always on the roads. In the ordinary business of life, Christians had journeys to make. Both their price and their moral atmosphere made the public inns impossible. In those days, there must have been many isolated Christians fighting a lonely battle for the faith. Christianity was, and still should be, the religion of the open door. The writer to the Hebrews says that those who have given hospitality to strangers have sometimes, without knowing it, entertained the angels of God. He is thinking of the time when the angel came to Abraham and Sarah to tell them of the coming of a son (Genesis 18:1ff.) and of the day when the angel came to Manoah to tell him that he would have a son (Judges 13:3ff.).

(3) There is *sympathy for those in trouble*. It is here we see the early Christian Church at its loveliest. It often happened that Christians ended up in prison and worse. It might be for their faith; it might be for debt, for the Christians were poor; it might be that they were captured by pirates or by bandits. It was then that the Church went into action.

Tertullian in *The Apology* writes: 'If there happen to be any in the mines, or banished to the islands, or shut up in prisons for nothing but their fidelity to the cause of God's Church, they become the nurslings of their confession.' Aristides the Athenian orator said of the Christians: 'If they hear that any one of their number is imprisoned or in distress for the sake of their Christ's name, they all render aid in his necessity and, if he can be redeemed, they set him free.' When Origen was young, it was said of him: 'Not only was he at the side of the holy martyrs in their imprisonment and until their final condemnation but, when they were led to death, he boldly accompanied them into danger.'

Sometimes, Christians were condemned to the mines – which was almost like being sent to Siberia in the former Soviet Union. *The Apostolic Constitutions* laid it down: 'If any Christian is condemned for Christ's sake to the mines by the ungodly, do not overlook him but from the proceeds of your toil and sweat send him something to support himself and to reward the soldier of Christ.' The Christians sought out their fellow Christians even in the remotest parts. There was actually a little Christian church in the mines at Phaeno.

Sometimes, Christians had to be ransomed from robbers and bandits. *The Apostolic Constitutions* laid it down: 'All monies accruing from honest labour do ye appoint and apportion to the redeeming of the saints ransoming thereby slaves and captives and prisoners, people who are sore abused or condemned by tyrants.' When the Numidian robbers carried off their Christian friends, the Church at Carthage raised sufficient money to ransom them and promised more. There were actually cases where Christians sold themselves as slaves to find money to pay the ransom for their friends.

They were even prepared to bribe their way into prison. The Christians became so notorious for their help to those in prison that, at the beginning of the fourth century, the Emperor Licinius passed new legislation that 'no one was to show kindness to sufferers in prison by supplying them with food and that no one was to show mercy to those starving in prison'. It was added that those who were discovered to be doing this kind of thing would be compelled to suffer the same fate as those they tried to help.

These instances are taken from Adolf von Harnack's book *The Expansion of Christianity*, and many others could be added. In the early days, no Christians who found themselves in trouble for the faith were ever neglected or forgotten by their fellow Christians.

(4) There is *purity*. First, the marriage bond is to be universally respected. This may mean either of two almost opposite things. (a) There were some people who despised marriage. Some even went to the lengths of castrating themselves to secure what they thought was purity. Origen, for instance, took that course. Even someone like Galen, the Greek physician, noted of the Christians that 'they include men and women who refrain from cohabiting all their lives'. The writer to the Hebrews insists against those who argued for abstinence that the marriage bond is to be honoured and not despised. (b) There were those who were always in danger of lapsing into immorality. The writer to the Hebrews uses two words.

The one denotes adulterous living; the other denotes all kinds of impurity and vice. The Christians brought into the world a new ideal of purity. Even the Greeks admitted that. Galen, in the passage we have already quoted, goes on: 'And they also number individuals who, in ruling and controlling themselves and in their keen pursuit of virtue, have attained a pitch not inferior to that of real philosophers.' When Pliny, the governor of Bithynia, examined the Christians and reported back to the Emperor Trajan, he had to admit, even though he was looking for a charge on which to condemn them, that at their Lord's Day meeting: 'They bound themselves by an oath not for any criminal end but to avoid theft or robbery or adultery, never to break their word nor repudiate a deposit when called upon to refund it.' In the early days, the Christians presented such a purity to the world that not even their critics and their enemies could find a fault in it.

(5) There is *contentment*. Christians must be free from the love of money. They must be content with what they have; and why should they not be, for they possess the continual presence of God? Hebrews quotes two great Old Testament passages – Joshua 1:5 and Psalm 118:6 – to show that those who belong to God need nothing more because they always have the presence and the help of God with them. Nothing that the world can give them can improve on that.

THE LEADERS AND THE LEADER

Hebrews 13:7–8

> Remember your leaders, the men who spoke the word of God to you. Look back on how they made their exit from this life, and imitate their faith. Jesus Christ is the same yesterday and today and forever.

IMPLICIT in this passage is a description of the real leader.

(1) The real leaders of the Church preach Christ and thereby bring others to him. The British Methodist pastor and broadcaster Leslie Weatherhead tells of a public school-boy who decided to enter the ministry. He was asked when he had come to that decision, and said it was after hearing a certain sermon in his school chapel. He was asked the name of the preacher, and his answer was that he had no memory of the preacher's name. All he knew was that he had shown him Jesus. The duty of real preachers is to obliterate self and show to those listening nothing but Christ.

(2) The real leaders of the Church live in the faith and thereby bring Christ to others. A saint has been defined as 'someone in whom Christ lives again'. The duty of real preachers is not so much to talk to men and women about Christ as to show them Christ in their own lives. People listen not so much to what they are saying as to what they are.

(3) The real leaders, if need be, die in loyalty. They show others how to live and are prepared to show them how to die. As the Gospel of John says, Jesus, having loved his own, loved them to the end (13:1); and real leaders, having loved Jesus, love him to the end. Their loyalty never stops halfway.

(4) As a result, real leaders leave two things to those who come after – an example and an inspiration. Quintilian, the Roman master of oratory, said: 'It is a good thing to know, and always to keep turning over in the mind, the things which were illustriously done of old.' Epicurus advised his disciples continuously to remember those who in the past had lived with virtue.

If there is one thing more than any other that the world and the Church need in every generation, it is leadership like that.

Then the writer to the Hebrews moves on to another great thought. It is in the nature of things that all earthly leaders must come and go. They have their part in the drama of life, and then the curtain comes down. But Jesus Christ is the same yesterday and today and forever. His status above all others is permanent; his leadership is forever. Therein lies the secret of earthly leadership; real leaders are people who are themselves led by Jesus Christ. That figure, who walked the roads of Galilee, is as powerful as ever to strike at evil and to love sinners; and, just as then he chose twelve to be with him and sent them out to do his work, so now he is still seeking those who will bring men and women to him and bring him to them.

THE WRONG AND THE RIGHT SACRIFICE

Hebrews 13:9–16

Do not let yourselves be carried away by subtle and strange teachings, for it is a fine thing to have your heart made strong by grace, not by the eating of different kinds of food, for they never did any good to those who took that line of conduct. We have an altar from which those who serve in the tabernacle have no right to eat. For the bodies of the animals, whose blood is taken by the High Priest into the Holy Place as an offering for sin, are burned outside the camp. That was why Jesus suffered outside the gate, so that he might make men fit for the presence of God by his own blood. So, then, let us go to him outside the camp, bearing the same reproach as he did, for here we have no abiding city but are searching for the city which is to come. Through him, therefore, let us continually bring to God a sacrifice of praise, I mean, the fruit of lips which continually acknowledge their faith in his name. Do not forget to do good and to share everything, for God is well pleased with a sacrifice like that.

IT may be that no one will ever discover the precise meaning behind this passage. Clearly, there was some false teaching going on in the church to which this letter was written. The writer to the Hebrews did not need to describe it; his readers knew all about it, because some of them had succumbed to it and all were in danger of it. As to what it was, we can only guess.

We may start with one basic fact. The writer to the Hebrews is convinced that real strength comes to a person's heart only from the grace of God and that what people eat and drink has nothing to do with their spiritual strength. So, in the church to which he was writing, there were some who placed too much importance on laws about food. There are certain possibilities.

(1) The Jews had rigid food laws, laid down at length in Leviticus 11. They believed they could serve and please God by eating and by not eating certain foods. Possibly there were some in this church who were ready to abandon their Christian liberty and once again put themselves under the burden of Jewish rules and regulations about food, thinking that by so doing they were going to add strength to their spiritual life.

(2) Some Greeks had very definite ideas about food. Long ago, Pythagoras had been like that. He believed in re-incarnation, that the soul of an individual passed from body to body until finally it gained release. That release could be hastened by prayer and meditation and self-discipline and abstinence; and so the Pythagoreans were vegetarians. There were people called Gnostics who were much the same. They believed that matter was altogether bad and that individuals

must concentrate on spirit, which is altogether good. They therefore believed that the body was altogether bad and that people ought to discipline their bodies and treat them with the greatest control and strictness. They cut down food to the bare minimum, and they, too, abstained from meat. There were any number of Greeks who thought that by what they ate or refused to eat they were strengthening their spiritual life and releasing their souls.

(3) Neither of these things seems quite to fit. This eating and drinking has something to do with the body of Jesus. The writer to the Hebrews goes back to the regulations for the Day of Atonement. According to these regulations, the body of the bullock which was an offering for the sins of the high priest and the body of the goat which was an offering for the sins of the people must be totally destroyed by fire in a place outside the camp (Leviticus 16:27). They were sin offerings, and the point is that even if the worshippers had wanted to eat their flesh they could not do so. The writer to the Hebrews sees Jesus as the perfect sacrifice. The parallel for him is complete because Jesus, too, was sacrificed 'outside the gate', that is, outside the city wall of Jerusalem. Crucifixions were always carried out outside a town. Jesus, then, was a sin offering for men and women; and it follows that, just as no one could eat the flesh of the sin offering on the Day of Atonement, no one can eat his flesh.

It may be that here we have the clue. There may have been a little group in this church who, either at the sacrament or at some common meal where they consecrated their food to Jesus, claimed that they were in fact eating the body of Christ. They may have persuaded themselves that, because they had consecrated their food to Christ, his body had entered into it. That was indeed what the religious Greeks believed about their gods. When the Greeks sacrificed, they were given back part of the meat. Often, they made a feast for themselves and their friends within the temple where the sacrifice had been made; and they believed that when they ate the meat of the sacrifice, the god to whom that meat had been sacrificed was in it and entered into them. It may well be that some Greeks had brought their own ideas with them into Christianity and talked about eating the body of Christ.

The writer to the Hebrews believed with all the intensity of his being that no food can bring Christ into a person and that Christ can enter into us only by grace. It is quite likely that we have here a reaction against an overstressing of the sacraments. It is a notable fact that the writer to the Hebrews never mentions the sacraments; they do not seem to come into his scheme at all. It is likely that, even at this early stage, there were those who viewed the sacraments as working in an almost mechanical way, forgetting that no sacrament in the world achieves anything by itself and that its only use is that in it the grace of God meets the faith of men and women. It is not the meat but the faith and the grace which matter.

This strange argument has set the writer to the Hebrews thinking. Christ was crucified outside the gate. He was exiled from society and numbered with criminals. In this, the writer to the Hebrews sees a picture. We, too, have to sever ourselves from the life of the world and be willing to bear the same reproach as Christ bore. The isolation and the humiliation may come to Christians as they came to their Saviour.

The writer to the Hebrews goes further. If Christians cannot again offer the sacrifice of Christ, what can they offer? The writer says they can offer certain things.

(1) They can offer their continual praise and thanks to God. The ancient peoples sometimes argued that a thank-offering was more acceptable to God than a sin offering; for, when people offered a sin offering, they were trying to get

something for themselves, while a thank-offering was the unconditional offering of grateful hearts. The sacrifice of gratitude is one that all may and should bring.

(2) They can offer their public and glad confession of faith in the name of Christ. That is the offering of loyalty. Christians can always offer to God lives that are never ashamed to show to whom they belong and whom they serve.

(3) Christians can offer acts of kindness to their neighbours. In fact, that was something with which Jews were familiar. After AD 70, the sacrifices of the Temple came to an end when the Temple was destroyed. The Rabbis taught that, with the Temple ritual gone, theology, prayer, penitence, the study of the law and charity were sacrifices equivalent to the ancient ritual. Rabbi Jochanan ben Zakkai comforted himself in those sorrowful days by believing that 'in the practice of charity he still possessed a valid sacrifice for sin'. An ancient Christian writer says: 'I expected that your heart would bear fruit and that you would worship God, the Creator of all, and unto him continually offer your prayers by means of compassion; for compassion shown to men by men is a bloodless sacrifice and holy unto God.' After all, Jesus himself said: 'Just as you did it to one of the least of these who are members of my family, you did it to me' (Matthew 25:40). The best of all sacrifices to bring to God is the gift of help to one of his children in need.

OBEDIENCE AND PRAYER

Hebrews 13:17–19

> Obey your leaders and submit to them, for they sleeplessly watch over your souls, conscious that they will have to give account of their trust. This do that

they may carry out this task with joy and not with grief, for, if you grieve them, there would be no profit to you either in that. Keep on praying for us, for we believe that we have a clear conscience, for we wish in all things to live in such a way that our conduct will be fair. I urge you to do this all the more that I may the more quickly be enabled to return to you.

THE writer to the Hebrews lays down the duty of the congregation to its present leaders and its absent leader.

To the present leaders, the duty of the congregation is obedience. A church is a democracy but not a democracy taken to extremes; it must give obedience to those whom it has chosen as its guides. That obedience is not to be given in order to gratify the leaders' sense of power or to increase their prestige. It is to be given so that at the end of the day the leaders may be seen to have lost none of the souls committed to their care. The greatest joy of the leaders of any Christian fellowship is to see those whom they lead established in the Christian way. As John wrote: 'I have no greater joy than this, to hear that my children are walking in the truth' (3 John 4). The greatest sorrow of the leaders of any Christian fellowship is to see those whom they lead growing further away from God.

To the absent leader, the duty of the congregation is that of prayer. It is a Christian duty always to bear our absent loved ones to the throne of God's grace and daily to remember there all who bear the responsibility of leadership and authority. When Stanley Baldwin became Prime Minister of Great Britain, his friends gathered round to congratulate him. He said: 'It is not your congratulations I need, it is your prayers.'

We must give our respect and our obedience to those set in authority over us in the Church when they are present with us, and when they are absent we must remember them in our prayers.

A PRAYER, A GREETING AND
A BLESSING

Hebrews 13:20–4

> May the God of peace, who brought up from among the dead the great shepherd of the sheep with the blood of the eternal covenant, it is our Lord Jesus I mean, equip you with every good thing that you may do his will, and may he create in you through Jesus Christ that which is well-pleasing in his sight. To him be glory forever and ever. Amen.
>
> Brothers, I appeal to you to bear with this appeal of mine, for indeed it is but a short letter that I have sent to you.
>
> I would have you know that our brother Timothy is at liberty again. If he comes soon, I will see you along with him.
>
> Greet all your leaders and all God's dedicated people. The folk from Italy send you their greetings. Grace be with you all. Amen.

THE great prayer of the first two verses of this passage draws a perfect picture of God and of Jesus.

(1) God is the God of peace. Even in the most disturbing and distressing situation, he can bring peace to our souls. In any fellowship where there is division, it is because people have forgotten God, and only remembering his presence can bring back the lost peace. When our minds and hearts are distracted and we are torn in two between the two sides of our own nature, it is only by giving our lives into the control of God that we can know peace. It is only the God of peace

who can make us at peace with ourselves, at peace with each other and at peace with him.

(2) God is the God of life. It was God who brought Jesus again from the dead. His love and power are the only things that can bring us peace in life and triumph in death. It was to obey the will of God that Jesus died; and that same will brought him again from the dead. For those who obey the will of God, there is no such thing as final disaster; even death itself is conquered.

(3) God is the God who both shows us his will and equips us to do it. He never gives us a task without also giving us the power to accomplish it. When God sends us out, he sends us equipped with everything we need.

The picture of Jesus is also threefold.

(1) Jesus is the great shepherd of his sheep. The picture of Jesus as the good shepherd is very precious to us; but, strangely enough, it is one that Paul never uses and that the writer to the Hebrews uses only here. There is a lovely legend of Moses which tells of something he did when he had fled from Egypt and was keeping the flocks of Jethro in the desert. A kid wandered far away from the flock. Moses patiently followed it and found it drinking at a mountain stream. He came up to it and put it on his shoulder. 'So it was because you were thirsty that you wandered away,' said Moses gently; and, without any anger at the toil the young goat had caused him, he carried it home. When God saw it, he said: 'If Moses is so compassionate to a straying kid, he is the very man I want to be the leader of my people.' A shepherd is one who is ready to give his life for his sheep; he puts up with their foolishness and never stops loving them. That is what Jesus does for us.

(2) Jesus is the one who established the new covenant and made possible the new relationship between God and all

people. It was he who took away the terror and showed us the love of God.

(3) Jesus is the one who died. To show us what God is like and to open the way to him, it cost the life of Jesus. Our new relationship to God cost his blood.

The letter finishes with some personal greetings. The writer to the Hebrews half-apologises for its length. If he had dealt with these vast topics, the letter would never have ended at all. It is short – James Moffatt points out that you can read it aloud in less than an hour – in comparison with the greatness of the eternal truths with which it deals.

What the reference to Timothy means, no one knows; but it sounds as if he, too, had been in prison because of Jesus Christ.

And so the letter closes with a blessing. All through, it has been telling of the grace of Christ which opens the way to God; and it comes to an end with a prayer that that wondrous grace may rest upon its readers.